T0419683

Battlefield
of the
mind

FOR TEENS

JOYCE MEYER
WITH TODD HAFER

Battlefield
of the
mind

WINNING THE BATTLE
IN YOUR MIND

Faith
Words

NEW YORK   NASHVILLE

FaithWords
Hachette Book Group
1290 Avenue of the Americas, New York, NY 10104
faithwords.com
twitter.com/faithwords

First published in June 2006
Revised Edition: March 2018

FaithWords is a division of Hachette Book Group, Inc. The FaithWords name and logo are trademarks of Hachette Book Group, Inc.

The publisher is not responsible for websites (or their content) that are not owned by the publisher.

The Hachette Speakers Bureau provides a wide range of authors for speaking events. To find out more, go to www.hachettespeakersbureau.com or call (866) 376-6591.

Library of Congress Cataloging-in-Publication Data has been applied for.

ISBNs: 978-1-5460-3325-7 (trade paperback), 978-0-7595-7386-4 (ebook)

Printed in the United States of America

LSC-C

Printing 7, 2020

CONTENTS

INTRODUCTION

Proverbs 23:7 tells us, "For as [a person] thinks in his heart, so is he" (NKJV). In other words, your thoughts determine your actions. Think of your body as a top-of-the line sports car. This car is designed with the latest technology and can reach top speeds. But what really controls this car? The person handling the steering wheel, the person pointing the car in a certain direction and pressing the accelerator or the brakes.

I believe that just as the steering wheel controls the direction of the car, the mind controls the direction of a person. Your actions are set by your mind. When you point your mind in a certain direction, your body follows through with actions. Regardless of how well you can perform, how fast you can go, or how sleek you may look, you won't do anything if your mind isn't pointed in the right direction. In fact, if your mind is going the wrong way, you're going to follow and end up at a dead end, too.

But there is great news: God has given us all of the tools we need to have our minds pointed on the path He'd like us to take. We just need to pick up those tools and activate them so we can steer in the right direction. We can win the battles raging in our minds.

I have helped so many people like you better understand God's Word, and the longer I serve Him and study His Word, the more I realize how important thoughts and words are. I truly believe there is a battle raging in your mind, because there was one raging inside of mine. And I don't want to just help you win, but win big!

Not only do I want you to win the battle for your mind, I want you to be able to help others win, too.

Let's look at another translation of Proverbs 23:7, which says: "As a man thinks in his heart, so does he become." Did you catch the subtle difference between the two translations? That's right, the battle for your mind not only decides who you are as a person right now—but also who you will be in the future.

Your life, your actions will always be a direct result of your thoughts. If you have a negative mind-set, you will have a negative life. But if you renew your mind according to God's plan for you, you will have a full and rewarding life. It's that simple.

Your life might be very difficult right now. Studies show that nearly all high-school students suffer from stress at least some of the time. But don't give up. Don't despair or become cynical. Little by little, you can change. The fact that you are reading these words right now shows that you realize you could use some help. And asking the right questions (for example, asking for help) is a great place to start.

But one thing you have to commit to right from the start is this: Never give up hope. Keep striving to change your mind for the better. Because when you change your mind for the better, you change your life for the better. When you begin to see God's amazing plan for your life, you'll want to follow it. I pray that this book will help you win the battle for your mind.

PART ONE

The Shifting Mind

INTRODUCTION

I have a question for you: Where's your mind right now? Were you in a different head space last week? Last year?

If you're like most people, your mental condition changes drastically and quickly. It can be as unpredictable as the weather. One day you might be calm and peaceful. A week later, you're uptight, anxious, and worried about almost everything.

Or have you ever made a decision such as signing up for a certain class in school or breaking up with a boyfriend or girlfriend, then immediately second-guessed yourself?

More important, have you felt great about your spiritual life—really close to God—for a while, then found yourself slipping? Unable to find the motivation to crack open your Bible? Making excuses for not attending church or youth group? Not praying unless you had some kind of emergency you wanted God to bail you out of?

I've been there, too. At some points in my life I seemed to be able to believe in God and trust His Word almost like it was second nature to me. But at other times, doubt and unbelief overwhelmed me. So, I began to ask myself, *What's wrong with me? Is my mind normal? And what, exactly, is normal, anyway?*

I had a judgmental, critical mind, something that was not in line with God and His Word. But since my mind had been this way for a major portion of my life, I figured it had to be normal, even though I questioned it at times. After all, it was what I was used to. Besides, as far as I knew then, there was nothing I could do to change my thought life. I was used to thinking negatively, so I figured I was stuck with this mind-set. I was stuck thinking this was just the way I'd be and just the way my life would be.

I want to emphasize that I had been a Christian for years at this point in my life, but no one had ever taught me about changing my thought life or given me standards for how my mind should function as a child of God. I was not living the fulfilling and abundant life Jesus promised in John 10:10.

Remember, our minds are not born again when we become Christians. Our minds have to be renewed, and this renewal is a process that requires time. So don't be discouraged or devastated when you read the next part of this book. You might discover that your mind isn't in the right condition. That's okay. Recognizing the problem is the first step to getting where you need to be.

Imagine an athlete who thinks he's in pretty good shape. He's worked out a bit during the summer and seems fit compared to most of his buddies. But he shows up for the first day of football practice and finds out that his forty-yard dash times are slow, or much slower than he thought they would be. At first, he can't even believe the stopwatch. He's not *that* slow.

But then he goes to the weight room, where he discovers he can't bench-press his body weight even once. This is not good news if he wants to have a good season. If this guy wants to be a successful football player, he now has some information on where he is physically versus where he needs to be. He is surprised by what he finds out, but the good news is that he knows something he didn't know before. Now he can deal with reality of what he needs to do to get into top shape.

In my case, my world got rocked several years ago when I began to get serious about my relationship with God. As I drew closer to Him, He began to reveal to me how so many of my problems were rooted in wrong thinking. In short, my mind was a mess! It's possible that it had never been in the condition it should have been.

This realization overwhelmed me and surprised me. I began to see that I was addicted to wrong thinking. I would try to fling out the bad thoughts when they came into my mind, but like boomerangs, they flew right back. If you or a friend have ever tried to break a bad habit but kept falling back into old ways, you already understand what I'm talking about.

It's just as hard to overcome wrong thinking, because the enemy will fight you aggressively during the process of renewing your mind. I'm certainly not trying to make this sound spooky or hyper-Christian, but we do have an enemy as followers of Christ, and that enemy is the devil. And because of it, we are all in a battle.

So you have to pray and study the Bible. You have to grab God's promises and live them out in your everyday life. You have to do whatever it takes to reclaim your mind. You'll be mentally wandering less and focusing more. You'll be less upset and confused and more sure of the direction your life is going. You'll be less afraid, because you'll realize that, as a child of God, you have the privilege of casting all your cares on Him.

So, prayerfully, get ready for the next part of this book. I believe it will open your eyes to mind-sets that are getting you into trouble and paint a picture of the right-minded follower of Jesus. It's time to win the battle for your mind.

Is My Mind Normal, or What?

But we have the mind of Christ
(the Messiah) and do hold the thoughts (feelings and
purposes) of His heart.
1 Corinthians 2:16 AMP

he Centers for Disease Control estimates that almost 39 percent of American adults are overweight and 18 percent of them are obese. So you might assume that being overweight is normal. It's not. Sure, the average person might be overweight these days, but that is not normal.

There is a distinction between average and normal, and it becomes even more important when we talk about the mind. When you ask yourself, *What condition should my mind be in?*, you can't just look at the people around you and compare yourself to them. You have to go deeper.

When we become Christians, the Holy Spirit takes up residence inside us. Now the Spirit knows God's mind, and one of His purposes is to reveal to us God's wisdom and guidance.

But our challenge is to understand what the Holy Spirit is trying to help teach us. As humans, we are a combo of the natural and the spiritual. The natural brain operates by natural laws—neurons firing, serotonin being released, and so on. The brain's natural functions help us process information, solve problems, and lots, lots more. But for all its wonders, our amazing natural brains don't understand spiritual stuff (see 1 Cor. 2:14).

To grasp the spiritual, the mind needs to be taught by the Holy Spirit. The problem is that our minds are often too busy thinking on other things to receive wisdom from the Holy Spirit. Worry, anxiety, and fear take up space in our mind, and we have no room for what God's Spirit is telling us to do. It's like we're out of storage space when it comes to the stuff that will help us. We've got to delete some things to make room for God's Spirit to reside in our minds.

In short, your mind is normal when it's at rest. When it is at rest and uncluttered with ongoing thoughts, you can be much more attentive to God.

Think about it for a minute: Is your mind usually, normally, serene and at rest? Or is it overloaded, bombarded with information, stress, demands, deadlines, and schedules? If you're feeling overwhelmed, you are not alone.

When was the last time you allowed your mind to just chill? When you took a moment to focus on God and His plan for your life?

The Holy Spirit stands by ready to help, but if your mind is too busy with other things, you might miss Him.

Are You Too Stressed for Success?

Based on a national survey, these are the top five stress-inducers for teens. How many of them do you experience?

1. Feeling overwhelmed by homework.
2. Not having enough money.
3. Wanting to do well on college placement tests.
4. Juggling multiple priorities.
5. Feeling fat/physically unattractive.

Big God, Small Voice

The Lord said [to Elijah], "Go out and stand on the mountain in the presence of the Lord, for the Lord is about to pass by." Then a great and powerful wind tore the mountains apart and shattered the rocks before the Lord, but the Lord was not in the wind. After the wind there was an earthquake, but the Lord was not in the earthquake. After the earthquake came a fire, but the Lord was not in the fire. And after the fire came a gentle whisper.
1 Kings 19:11–12

Have you experienced anything like Elijah did in this passage? Have you ever prayed for wisdom from God, but He answered in a way you didn't expect?

For years, I prayed for God to show me what to do with my life and how I was supposed to act. I knew that my requests were in line with the Bible. I felt sure I should be asking God to reveal things to me, and I felt sure I would get an answer.

But instead, a lot of the time I felt like I just couldn't hear Him. Then, finally, I learned that I wasn't catching much of what the Holy Spirit was throwing my way because my mind was too frantic and busy.

Imagine you're at a loud concert with your best friend and in the middle of the loudest part, you whisper something. Not only are you going to go unheard, but unless your friend happens to look at you, she might not even know you're saying anything at all.

That's the way it is with the communication from God's Spirit to our hearts and minds. The ways of the Spirit are gentle. Most of the time, He speaks to us just as in Elijah's case, in a still, small voice. That's why it's vital to keep our minds tuned in to listening for His Voice.

Isaiah 26:3 promises, "You will guarded him and keep him in perfect and constant peace whose mind [both its inclination and its character] is stayed on You, because he commits himself to You, leans on You, and hopes confidently in You" (AMP).

Commit to keeping your mind set on God. The enemy is going to try to overload you and overwork your mind by filling it with destructive and just plain meaningless thoughts. You must keep your mind open and available to God's Spirit. Again, keep your mind set on Jesus. A mind stayed on Him is a mind at rest and at peace.

CHAPTER 2

Where Is My Mind?

n the previous chapter, we learned that a "busy" mind is not
normal. But there are other things that can make the mind
abnormal, too. In this chapter, we'll go through a couple more.

How many times has this happened to you? You're sitting in
a class at school, and, for a while, you are tuned in to everything
the teacher is saying. You're absorbing the information and even
taking notes. Then, for some reason, your mind decides to take a

little trip, maybe to a friend's house weekend plans or across the country to visit a cousin.

After a while, the lecture starts coming through again, but you look at your watch and realize that, mentally speaking, you were somewhere else for the past twelve minutes.

This has happened to me, too—even at church. It's something common to all of us. Mind wandering is average, but it's not normal.

Too many people spend years allowing their minds to wander off. That's because they've never applied the principles of discipline to their thought life. They would never let a child, a younger sibling, or even a pet wander off to who knows where, but they do it with their thoughts all the time. After a while, it can become a bad habit.

I think people who can't seem to concentrate quite often think they are mentally deficient. And I believe God has given us mental and physical health professionals for us to use when we need help. While some should utilize the medical professionals God has given us, if that seems an appropriate course of action, many times people who can't concentrate just lack discipline. After years of letting the mind gallop off to do what it wants to, it's hard to rein it back in. It takes practice. It takes discipline to change your thought patterns.

Another reason people find it hard to concentrate is that they lack proper nutrition. In particular, B-vitamins enhance the ability to concentrate. So if you are plagued by an inability to focus, it might be worth a trip to a doctor or nutritionist.

Another big factor associated with poor concentration is fatigue. Have you ever lost track of time playing games or texting late on a school night, then found it was virtually impossible to pay attention in class the next day?

I have found that when I get overtired, the enemy will try to attack my mind, because he knows it's more difficult for me to resist him when I'm worn-down.

Your mind can wander when you read, too. I can read a chapter in the Bible, get to the end, then realize that I don't have any idea about what I just read. I go back and read the chapter again, and it all seems new to me. This is because, even though my eyes were scanning the words on the pages, my mind had gone somewhere else. It wasn't alert and available to process what I was reading. Because I failed to focus, I failed to comprehend.

In the book of Ecclesiastes, the wise man Solomon advises people to "give your mind to what you are doing" (5:1 AMP). Think about that advice. It means to commit your mind to the words on the page, the words in the song, or from your parents or teachers. This is what a speaker means when they say, "Give me your full attention."

The full attention thing has not been easy for me. I used to have a wandering mind, and I had to train it by discipline. The training was not easy, and I confess that I still struggle sometimes. In defining the word *wander*, the dictionary uses words like "move about aimlessly" and "amble." I can be writing a book and suddenly realize that I'm thinking about something that has nothing to do with the book or its topic.

I have definitely not arrived at a place of perfect concentration all the time, but at least now I understand how important it is to guard my mind from "moving about aimlessly" wherever it wishes, whenever it desires. And I'm aware of my tendency, so I'm more on guard about it.

Simply being aware can make a big difference. In conversations with my husband, Dave, I used to listen for a while, then take a little mental vacation and miss huge chunks of what he was saying. There was a time when I would try to cover up my inattentiveness, nod affirmatively, and pretend I caught every single word. This was disrespectful as well as dishonest. I may have missed some really important things, which can cause major disagreements.

Now, when my mind wanders—and I admit that it still does once in a while—I stop Dave and say, "Can you repeat what you just said? I'm sorry, but I let my mind wander off, and I missed it."

It can be embarrassing to admit that you spaced out, but in the end it's much more respectful to someone than to have faked hearing. And you won't have to miss out on a key piece of information or suffer the deeper embarrassment when asked a question like, "Do you agree with what I just said?" or "How does that plan sound to you?"

Being honest like this also shows people that you recognize you have a tendency and you're confronting it and working on it. And confronting a problem is the only way to defeat it.

Another way to battle a wandering mind is to find ways to reinforce the messages God is trying to communicate to you. Downloading sermons or podcasts can keep your mind fixed on God's Word. Listening to these on your way to school or work or while working out is a great way to reflect on key points or catch something you might have missed at church.

If you are studying a book of the Bible, try reading passages in a couple of different versions of the Bible (Bible software and apps can help you read different versions easily). I've used this technique in this book. Sometimes, the different ways of phrasing a concept broaden and deepen our understanding of it.

Music is another great way to ward off a wandering mind.

The rhythm, rhymes, and beat of a song can help you remember a Bible verse or key biblical truth.

A Wondering Mind

In addition to keeping your wandering mind in check, it's also good to realize you have to keep your wondering mind in check as well. And I should point out that I'm not talking about the kind of awe-filled wonder we feel toward God and His creation. This is wonder of another sort...

"I wonder what kind of grades I'll get this semester."

"I wonder if I'll get a good job someday."

"I wonder when I will get married."

"I wonder how old I'll live to be."

Have you ever thought about stuff like this? For me, my "wonders" are things like, "I wonder how my son is handling the pressure at his work," or "I wonder how many people will show up at the conference I'm teaching, and I wonder what I should wear."

These kinds of statements reflect the idea of wonder that's defined as "a feeling of puzzlement or doubt."

If your mind is in a constant state of this kind of wonder, that's not normal. It's just a waste of time, and it stirs up unnecessary worry. I have found that I am much better off doing something positive rather than just wondering about things all the time.

For example, instead of wondering how my son is doing, I can pray for him, encourage him, and help him if he needs it. And instead of fretting over conference attendance, I can prepare well, commit to doing my best, then turn the matter over to the Lord and trust Him to work out all things for good, regardless of who or how many show up.

The "puzzlement" brand of wondering breeds indecision, and indecision causes confusion. And this state of mind prevents us from receiving from God, by faith, His answers and direction for our lives. Isn't it a better idea to have your mind focusing on good and faithful things rather than wondering about something you have no control over?

Note that in Mark 2:23–24, Jesus does not say, "Whatever you ask for in prayer, wonder if you will get it." Instead, He says, "Whatever you ask for in prayer, believe that you will receive it."

As Christians, we are sometimes called believers, and that's because we are supposed to believe, not doubt!

Your Mind, Your Battle

For our struggle is not against flesh and blood, but against
the rulers, against the authorities, against the powers of
this dark world and against the spiritual forces of evil in
the heavenly realms.
Ephesians 6:12 NIV

Now that we've gone through some of the practical ways your mind gets sidetracked, and how you can get too busy and not think about what you're thinking about, let's return to the topic of the battle we're all in.

As I said earlier, as Christians we *do* have an enemy, and it is the devil. His sole purpose is to distract and derail you from the life God has planned for you. He will do whatever it takes to get you focused on everything that is wrong with you and the ways you constantly fail. He will remind you that you aren't good enough and don't have what it takes to be a follower of Christ. These are just some of the thoughts he'll send your way. But he's a liar, and liars lie—**period**. In fact, Jesus called him "the father of lies and of all that is false" (John 8:44 AMP).

However, most importantly, there's something awesome to keep in mind: You've got God on your side. You're not going through this alone. And though there is a battle, the powerful truth is that with God—you win!

And to cripple His power from the start, here are some of the lies you're likely familiar with:

1. You don't need to listen to your parents, your pastor, your youth leaders, and all those other people who try to tell you how to live. I mean, look at 'em, those incompetent hyp- ocrites. Look at all their flaws and inconsistencies. This is your life. Live it your way. You only live once!

2. Drinking, drugs, and sex won't really hurt you. Nothing bad comes from them. It's just a big scare tactic. Adults just don't want you to have any fun—even though they had plenty when they were your age. They just want to control you. But hey, you should live your life—you only live once!

3. Do you really believe in "the devil" anyway? Get real—that's just a myth! There is no devil, and there is no hell. And, by the way, there is no God or heaven, either. "Right now" is all there is. So get yours while you can. And enjoy life.

4. Come on, admit it: You have doubts about God all the time. If God was real, why would He allow those doubts to creep up inside your head?

5. If there really was a God who cared, would you feel as lonely as you do, as overwhelmed by life as you do, as powerless to

change things? And would this God allow so much bad to happen?

Have you ever felt like someone was planting questions and concerns like these in your mind? That's how the enemy works. He plants all kinds of nagging thoughts, suspicions, and doubts in your mind. He moves slowly, according to the ways he thinks will trip you up the most. And he's going to attack you where you're weak and where you're inconsistent.

For example, he knows your insecurities. If you are self-conscious about your body, someone may come into your life who tells you that you're hot, someone who makes you feel attractive. Then, this person you've welcomed into your life might start to pressure you to have sex. You know you want to wait until it's the person God has chosen for you to marry, but you don't want to risk losing someone right now who makes you feel so good about yourself.

He also knows that you can't turn on the TV, your computer, or a phone without seeing sexual content of some sort. (For example, there are more than 4 million pornographic websites on the Internet and many other images floating through social media.) He'll invest as much time as it takes to bring you down.

Fortunately for you, you're not going into the battle unarmed. The Bible, God's Word, assures you, "For the weapons of our warfare are not physical [weapons of flesh and blood], but they are mighty before God for the overthrow and destruction of strongholds, [Inasmuch as we] refute arguments and theories and reasonings and every proud and lofty thing that sets itself up against the [true] knowledge of God; and we lead every thought and purpose away captive into the obedience of Christ (the Messiah, the Anointed one)" (2 Corinthians 10:4–5 AMP).

Now you might be asking yourself, what are "strongholds," and how am I supposed to overthrow and destroy them? Think of it this way: Satan wants to keep you distracted by making you focus on the areas where you are weak.

Let's say you are struggling to overcome a painful situation that happened in your past. Maybe like me, you endured abuse. And because of it, you don't feel like you are worthy of love— real love, the pure, God-type of love. The enemy wants to keep you focused on how ugly you are, how gross you feel about what happened. He may even convince you that it was somehow your fault.

After a while, you start to believe the lie—you start to live and act like it's true. And even though it's a lie, you've started to think it's true, and because of it, it's holding you as a prisoner.

To overthrow or destroy this "stronghold," you have to go to God and ask Him what He thinks about it. What does God's Word say about you? What does He say about you? To Him you are lovely, you are worth more to Him than you could ever image. His very breath is inside of you. He knit you together in your mother's womb and knows the number of hairs on your head.

Of course, this is just one example. The same kind of thing happens with any situation. Instead of focusing on God's Word and how He wants us to live, the enemy would rather we take our eyes off those truths and instead fixate on his lies. Regardless of what you are dealing with—lying to others because you feel insecure about yourself, cheating on tests at school, addiction to drugs or alcohol—the enemy is trying to derail you, because he knows that once you see with the clarity of God's Word, you are unstoppable.

**10 Additional Examples of the Ways Teens Are
Struggling with the Battle for Their Minds**

1. Almost half of all ninth through twelfth-graders have had sex—including 61 percent of high-school seniors; and teens who watch lots of sex on TV and in movies are more than twice as likely to have sex as those who are more discerning about their entertainment choices (according to *Christian Retailing* and Rand.org).

2. Alcohol is the most commonly abused drug of all by underage youth in the U.S. Excessive drinking is the cause of more than 4,300 deaths among youth each year, according to the Centers for Disease Control (CDC).

3. Seventy-three percent of teens say they see at least one act of discrimination a month, but only 22 percent speak up and do something about it ("Racism Today," *Seventeen* magazine).

4. Parents and teens are not on the same page—or even in the same book—when it comes to sex. While half of today's teens are sexually active, 84 percent of parents believe their kids are not sexually active. Meanwhile, 87 percent of teens say it would be easier to delay sex if they could have more open, honest talks with parents, according to a teenpregnancy.org survey.

5. One in six of today's young females is drunk when she loses her virginity. One in seven say their partner was drunk, as well, also according to a teenpregnancy.org survey.

6. While the teen-pregnancy rate in the U.S. has steadily declined over the past twenty years, the U.S. still has more teens having babies than any other developed country; in fact the rate is nine times higher, according to the CDC.

7. Suicide was named the third leading cause of death among Americans ages fifteen to twenty-four according to a National Adolescent and Young Adult Health Information Center (NAHIC) survey.

8. About one in four sexually active teens has contracted a sexually transmitted disease, according to the Minnesota Department of Health statistics.

9. About nineteen kids a day in the U.S. are hospitalized or die due to gunshot wounds (CDC).

10. The average age at which teens start taking drugs is thirteen, said the Partnership for a Drug-Free America.

Okay, let's take a look at what we've learned so far.

1. We are all in a war inside our minds.

2. The devil is your enemy.

3. He will first try and convince you he doesn't even exist.

4. He will attack you where you are weak and where you have insecurities.

5. He will exploit those weaknesses and insecurities and try and convince you of his lies, but none of it is true, because he is a liar.

6. God is on your side, and He not only wants to set you free from these "strongholds" but remind you of your worth and value and that He has an incredible plan for your life.

John, Mary, and the Blended Family That Doesn't Wanna Blend

Every family has its problems, but a teen named Mary and her stepfather feel like their family suffers from more drama and trauma than the hottest reality show. Here are their two sides of the same sad story.

Mary's Got a Problem: "My stepdad is totally ruining my life!"

Mary's biological mom divorced Mary's bio-dad and remarried a man named John two years later. Seventeen-year-old Mary and her new dad are always fighting. She resents him because his presence killed all hopes of Mary's mom and "real dad" getting back together.

She's so angry all the time that she cannot concentrate in school, and her stomach gets upset every time she tries to eat. Her solution: Don't eat, unless she feels like she's going to pass out.

Mary doesn't want John to run her life. She resents his curfews and his strict punishments. He even tries to influence how she spends her money, which she earns by doing household chores. She wants him to "back off!"—which is exactly what she screams at him all of the time.

At this point, some of you might be thinking, *Whoa, Mary really needs help.* Has she tried a relationship with Jesus? The problem is she did that—when she was twelve. She was sincere about her decision to accept Jesus as her Savior. She believes she's going to heaven, and her anger toward her stepdad makes her feel guilty and sad. She does see hope for her life, but that hope seems a long way off. She thinks she will just have to get through this time at home with her mom and John and then get her freedom. But as she waits for that freedom, she admits she's "just plain miserable. "

Deep down, Mary knows her attitude is wrong. She wants to change. She has spent hours in counseling with her youth pastor and has even gone to the counselor at school. She prays about her struggle every night. She is bewildered about why she hasn't seen any lasting improvement in the situation. Why isn't this getting better?" she sobs to herself one night. "I'm so tired of feeling miserable all the time."

The solution to Mary's problem can be found in Romans 12:2: "Do not conform any longer to the pattern of this world, but be transformed by the renewing of your mind. Then you will be able to test and approve what God's will is—his good, pleasing and perfect will."

You see, Mary's mind is being held prisoner by strongholds. Some have been there since she first heard the word *divorce* uttered in her house. She knows she shouldn't harbor the bitter, resentful thoughts about her stepfather, but she can't seem to get them out of her head.

Mary can't control her tantrums, her blatant disregard for "house rules," and her hateful words, because she can't control the thoughts behind them. She can't remove the strongholds that the devil has planted in her mind. Satan has constructed effective lies. All through the divorce proceedings, Mary became angrier and angrier at the situation.

But she didn't want to direct her anger at her biological parents, because she adored them both. She didn't want to think that two people she respected so much could be responsible for a situation that was tearing her insides apart. And she wouldn't let go of her desire for her parents to be together, even though they had made the decision to part.

And that's when the lies started: "You, Mary, are the reason behind the divorce. They fight because of you. You cost them a lot of money. They worry about your grades. You make them stressed out, and that's why they fight."

And there were other lies, too: "I bet that your parents have fallen out of love. Your mom wishes she had married someone else. Your dad feels the same way. I bet they cheated on each other long before the divorce."

As a result, Mary resolved a couple of things in her mind:

1. "If my behavior broke up one marriage, it can do it again. If I can make John totally miserable, maybe he'll leave, and my real mom and dad can be together again."
2. "I bet John was hitting on my mom back when she was still married to Dad. He's slimy. He should have just left us alone. Now I'm gonna make him pay! He'll wish he never came near my family."

Imagine all the lies playing in Mary's head, month after month, on a continuous loop, lies that deepen Mary's resentment toward John and her obsession with breaking up a marriage. Is it any wonder she's not the sweet, adoring daughter she once was? How can Mary pull herself out of her misery? What would you do if you were in her place?

Unleash Your Weapons

"If you abide in My word [hold fast to My teachings and live in accordance with them], you are truly My disciples. And you will know the Truth, and the Truth will set you free.
John 8:31–32 AMP

In this verse, Jesus tells us how we can come against the lies and negative feelings and instead hold onto what is true: We must absorb the knowledge of God's truth into our minds and hearts, renewing our minds with the wisdom and power of His Word.

God's Word, the Bible, is our arsenal, containing all the weapons we need to win the crucial battle for our minds. When we repeat God's word and really let it sink in, we have power and wisdom to think godly thoughts—to think as God would have us to think.

One of the great things about being alive in these times is the number of sources for acquiring the truth of God's Word. We have websites, Bible apps, Christian music, youth groups, youth conferences, guest speakers, radio and TV stations, instructional podcasts, and books. These resources make it possible to "abide" in God's Word—that means keep absorbing it and applying it in your life all of the time.

Need a couple more weapons? Try worship and prayer. Worship defeats the devil every time. He can't stand to hear it. But this praise must be real, from the heart. You can't go through the motions—raise your hands just to mimic someone else or mindlessly mouth the words.

The same thing goes with prayer. It's gotta be real—sincere. Some people breeze through the Lord's Prayer without even thinking about what they are saying. God doesn't want you to simply repeat words. He wants words to spring from the depths of your heart. He wants you to believe what you say and focus on him as you pray. And He wants prayers inspired by your close relationship with Him.

You should approach God in prayer as your loving Father. He adores you. He is full of mercy, and He wants to help you. Think about that: Some people help you out of duty or guilt or so that you will help them someday. Not God. He really wants to help you. He would absolutely love the opportunity to help you.

Next, get to know Jesus. Go through the Bible and read the

Scriptures in red—that color indicates Jesus said the words out of his mouth. Read every single word Jesus said. You'll learn that Jesus is your wise and true Friend. He loves you so much that He died for you. Finally, get to know God's Holy Spirit living inside you.

God's Spirit can help you pray even when you can't find the right words, or any words at all. The Spirit can translate the deepest feelings in your soul—feelings you can't put into words or even describe—and convey them to God the Father. And if you're not sure if the Holy Spirit is in you, just know that if you've accepted Jesus, the Holy Spirit is already inside you. All you have to do is recognize Him and ask for His help.

If you would like some inspiration and instruction on prayer, the Bible is full of them. Check out Psalms, for example. This book of the Bible provides dozens of prayers—from heartfelt praises, to anguished cries for help, to dead-honest confessions of sin.

Mary needs to use these weapons. As she approaches God in prayer, she will be able to take a sledgehammer to all those strongholds in her mind. The truth of God's Word and the reality of His power will set her free.

She will see the truth: That her stepdad is probably doing the best he can to be a good father to her and a good husband to her mom. That living as a blended family isn't easy, and that everyone needs to show mercy and understanding and compassion to everyone else. That tantrums and disobedience aren't the way to bring about positive change. Her parents want the best for her, and she needs to listen to them. She is making herself miserable, and she won't get free until she changes her mind and attitude.

John's Got a Problem: "My stepdaughter won't give me a chance!"

Now, let's take a look at another key player in this family drama. Just because John is an adult doesn't mean that he isn't part of the problem.

John wants to be the strong leader of his family, but Mary is wearing him down. He's tired of the screaming matches, the slamming doors, and the mean stares. He's grown weary of setting up boundaries that Mary is going to ignore anyway. Lately, he just comes home from work, turns on the TV, and lapses into a sports coma.

John is hiding from his responsibility, because, at heart, he hates confrontation—especially when nothing good seems to come from it. He has begun telling himself, "Well, if I just stay off of Mary's case for a while, our problems will work themselves out. In time, she'll come to accept me. Of course, I'll keep praying about it, but beyond that, what can I do?"

Did you catch that last part? John is excusing himself from taking real action, and he's using prayer as an excuse. Now you've already read that prayer is a great weapon for battling the enemy—but not if it's used as an excuse for shrugging off responsibility. If you misuse prayer like this, it stops being effective.

At this point in the John/Mary saga, I should clarify what I mean when I say that John should assume his God-given position in the home. I don't mean that he should try to be a bully and force change by any means necessary. The Bible teaches that a man should love his family in the same way that Christ loves His people, the Church. And Christ was an effective leader, but He was also a humble servant. He put others' needs ahead of His own comfort.

So, like Christ, John needs to take firm, loving responsibility for his family, including Mary. He should reassure her that even though the divorce has been painful to her, she can throw herself into God's loving arms and trust that her stepdad is doing his best to be a loving, responsible parent to her. John also needs to assure her that he had nothing to do with the divorce—that he came along after the fact and is just trying to be the best husband and parent he can.

John's task isn't easy. Like Mary, he also has territory in his mind that has become occupied by fear, doubt, and the pain of his past. John was verbally abused as a child. His domineering mother had a sharp tongue and frequently said things like, "John, you are such an incompetent mess. How do you expect to ever get a good job and be a good husband and father, huh? You're a slacker, and you're never going to get anywhere in life."

John tried hard to please his mom, because he craved her approval. But the harder he tried, the more mistakes he made. He had a habit of being clumsy, so his mother told him all the time that he was stupid.

His clumsiness and poor self-esteem made it hard for him to make friends. Then, in high school, there was a girl he really liked. They had a few dates, but she ended up dumping him for another guy, one who practically glowed with confidence and competence.

Every rejection, harsh word, and disappointment became another painful wound in John's mind. Soon, he had no courage or optimism for life. He became shy, quiet, and withdrawn. He tried to adapt to life by being as low-key as possible. He told himself, *There's no point in telling people what you're thinking or what you want, because they won't listen anyway. If you want people to accept you, you better go along with whatever they want.*

Sure, when he first became a parent, John tried to stand his ground and fulfill his responsibilities, but Mary only hated him for it. She attacked him verbally, just as his mother used to do. He became afraid that he would "lose" Mary, just like his friends and high-school girlfriend, so he eventually gave up. At least if I give Mary what she wants, he reasoned, she'll quit screaming at me. Besides, I'm not going to win in this situation anyway, so why make things miserable in the process? John gave in to the "easy" way out. He stopped trying to do things with Mary, and in some ways, he too waited for the day she would just grow up and move away.

Can you imagine what John and Mary's home life is like? Can you picture the strife? Many times, strife is an angry undercurrent in a home. Everyone knows it's there, but nobody wants to deal with it—or even acknowledge its existence.

This home's atmosphere is bleak, and everything feels chaotic.

What do you think will happen to Mary, and her mom and stepdad—three well-meaning Christian people trapped in a battle zone? Will they make it? It would be a shame to see another marriage fail and another family fall to ruin, or for Mary to make rash decisions just so she can leave the home and have her "freedom." Even as young adults, we need our parents. And that relationship can set the tone for other relationships in our lives. Learning how to express our feelings, forgiving others, and following rules are all important throughout life—not just when we are teens. If you get these practices down now, you'll have less trouble handling them in the future.

Mary and her stepfather can make it, but it won't be up to a family counselor or their pastor. It's up to the family. They will need to take John 8:31 and 32 to heart. ("If you hold to my teaching, you are really my disciples. Then you will know the truth, and the truth will set you free.") They will need to continue to study God's Word to discern His truth. Then they will need to act on that truth to set them free from their destructive patterns. They will all have to confront their pasts and realize why they feel and act the way they do.

It's painful to face our pasts, our faults, then deal with them. It just seems easier to justify our misbehavior and negative attitudes. Many people allow their pasts—how they were raised, things that happened to them, etc.—to pollute the rest of their lives. This doesn't work, and it's not fair to the people in our lives. Like some of you, I was abused when I was young. I was abused emotionally, verbally, and sexually. So I understand that the past might explain why we suffer. But we can't use the past as an excuse to stay in bondage to a negative, defeatist approach to life. If we do, the enemy wins. We let what was done to us win. But we miss out on the wonderful promises of Jesus.

Jesus stands ready to set you free. He will lead you to freedom in any area of your life, if only you're willing to follow Him. Like I've said before, I am living proof of that truth.

A Winnable War

No temptation has seized you except what is common to man. And God is faithful; he will not let you be tempted beyond what you can bear. But when you are tempted, he will also provide a way out.
1 Corinthians 10:13

I hope that the story of John and Mary shows you how the enemy can use our life circumstances to build strongholds in our minds, to invade our minds one thought at a time.

Thank God that we have weapons to fight the strongholds of

our minds. God won't abandon us in the heat of battle. Remember always the truth of I Corinthians 10:13: God won't ever let you be overmatched in battle. You will be able to bear any temptation tossed your way. God will always provide a way out of trouble—an escape route for you. Practice praying each time you're tempted to think you're a victim or in a no-win situation. Then look for ways God is providing help for you.

No matter what battle you're facing now or what might come your way in the future, God is on your side. And that means you can't lose. That's good news and reason to celebrate.

What Are You Thinking About?

For as he thinks in his heart, so is he...
Proverbs 23:7 NKJV

Think about the words in that verse; it's one of the most important verses in the entire Bible! That's why you'll see it sprinkled throughout this book. Your thoughts are powerful. They aren't just images and attitudes in your head; they determine who you are and who you are going to become. Given this reality, shouldn't you make thinking the right kind of thoughts a top priority in your life?

In this chapter, I want you to think about the importance of getting your thought life in sync with God's Word. Because here is an absolute truth about life: You can't live a positive life if you have a negative mind.

Romans 8:5 warns us, "Those who live according to the sinful nature have their minds set on what that nature desires; but those who live in accordance with the Spirit have their minds set on what the Spirit desires."

Let me put this truth another way: If your mental road map is filled with negativity, greed, lust, and pride, you will not be able to follow the path that God has laid out for your life's journey. You are going to stumble down, run into dead ends, and take detours that will lead you to disaster.

As I said in the very beginning of this book, your mind is like the steering wheel of your life; the thoughts you think guide you down the path of life. While positive thinking won't make everything perfect in your life, it will give you a helpful perspective and help you recognize and enjoy God's promises more.

Do you see people around you whose lives seem to be a perpetual mess? Do a few of your friends fit into this category? Maybe it's a brother or sister. People try to help them; maybe they try to help themselves, but they just can't make any consistent progress. If so, it is probably because their efforts are well meant but ultimately ineffective. For example, if someone is addicted to meth, those around him might think that if they can control his access to the drug, things will be okay. This approach might help for a while, but addicts are crafty and resourceful. If they really want to find drugs, they probably will.

The only way to truly help someone like this is to get his mind straightened out; then his life will follow. You have to get to the root of the problem, not just deal with the visible results.

I'll give you a sneak preview of an interview you'll read later in this chapter. The interview features Terrence, a young man who was once addicted to drugs. As he tells of how he destroyed this particular issue in his life, he explains that he didn't merely quit using drugs. He says, "I became a new person. I became the kind of person who wouldn't use drugs."

He changed his whole way of thinking, his entire attitude toward life and drugs. That's why he is drug-free today, while so many others are trapped in a heartbreaking cycle of rebound/ relapse/repeat.

I learned a valuable lesson years ago. I was trying to grow closer to the Lord through praying and reading and studying the Bible. I was having a terrible time disciplining myself to do these things; I couldn't sit still to read or pray until God showed me how important these things are to life. He showed me that just as my physical life depends on nourishment, exercise, and proper medical care, my spiritual life thrives on spending regular, high-quality time with God.

By helping me understand this parallel between physical and spiritual well-being, God helped me learn to make my prayer time and Bible study time a priority. I realized that I needed time with God, just like my body needed food. Now I have a whole different attitude toward maintaining and growing my spiritual life. I wouldn't ignore the pangs of physical hunger, because I understand that eating isn't just a "routine" that I feel like I should go through; it's something I need. Feeding myself spiritually is vital, too. In fact, it's more important than the physical. After all, as it's been said, we are not human beings having a spiritual experience; we are spiritual beings having a human experience.

The War on Drugs, A Front-Line Interview

Check out the rest of the interview with Terrence, a young man who was once addicted to drugs. Note the mind-set that got him into drugs—and the one that helped him find a way out. Think about how the opening Scripture applies to each part of Terrence's story: "For as he thinks in his heart, so is he…" (Proverbs 23:7 NKJV).

How did you get addicted to drugs in the first place?

It was like falling down a hole. It happened so fast that I didn't even realize I was falling. One minute, I was at a party, listening to some music with a few new friends; the next minute I was desperate—doing things I never thought I'd do in a million years—all for the next high. There was no hideous thing I wouldn't do. Within weeks, I hated drugs. I hated getting high, but I had to.

What was drug addiction like?

It was like a trap, and I felt so stupid because I walked into it willingly. I was a smart kid. I knew the dangers. But I chose them anyway. I thought, Other guys can't handle it, but I'm smart. I'm strong. I can stop. I'll be careful. I'll be able to control it. And then, as soon as I started using, I knew I'd been taken.

So, you lost control?

I never really had control from the moment I chose to step over the line and get messed up for the first time. You don't want to panic, so you tell yourself, It's cool. This isn't so bad. I'm just like all these other people. But the truth is you're dying and you know it, like, ten seconds after you start. And that's about nine seconds too late.

How did you stop doing drugs?

I didn't just stop using drugs. I became a new person. I'm still becoming that person every day, actually. I can't stop running in the opposite direction from [drugs] or it just might catch me. God has helped me a lot to change my identity. I said I was a Christian before I got into drugs, but I wasn't living it. I wasn't a new creation. I'd say anyone out there, if you have an addiction or a bad habit, don't just stop the behavior; change your whole identity. Become somebody else, someone who would never do the destructive things you are doing. Change your friends if they're into drugs. I did. I changed jobs, locations, habits, my thinking, the way I talked and dressed. Anything that fed my old ways.

What would you say to readers who are thinking of experimenting, or trying drugs "just once."

I thought just one little time wouldn't hurt. That one time led to thousands of wasted dollars, one hospitalization, almost dying, and years of regret. One little time won't hurt? I have just one word for that: OUCH!

Is Your Fruit Ripe?

In the gospel of Matthew, Jesus explained that a tree is known by its fruit. A diseased tree is going to bear bad fruit. An immature or malnourished tree won't bear any fruit at all.

The same principle rings true in our lives. Thoughts bear fruit. Think good thoughts, and the fruit of your life will be good. Think bad thoughts, and the fruit in your life will be bad.

You can take note of someone's attitude and demeanor toward life and know what kind of thinking is behind it. A sweet, kind person is not filled with mean, vindictive thoughts. By the same token, a truly evil person doesn't spend every waking hour dwelling on pure, loving thoughts.

Memorize Proverbs 23:7, perhaps in one or more Bible translations. One of my favorites is from the New American Standard Bible, which says, "For as he thinks within himself, so he is." But whichever version you prefer, hold on to the core message of this verse and let it be a guiding force in your life. As you think you are in your heart, so you will be. In other words, see it, then be it.

Perseverance
Pays Off

Let us not become weary in doing good for at the proper
time we will reap a harvest if we do not give up.
Galatians 6:9

ight now, you might think your life stinks. You might feel
lonely; you might feel rejected. Perhaps you're struggling
in school or feeling angry about your life and circumstances. Maybe, like me, you've been a victim of abuse by someone (like my father) whom you thought you could trust, and you
don't know how to deal with your feelings of guilt, betrayal, and
worthlessness. I'm here to tell you one thing: Don't give up!

No matter how badly your life is messed up and out of

control, you can take back the joy that has been taken from you. Or maybe you've never experience true joy. You can. You might regain (or gain) joy an inch at a time, but, by leaning on God's grace and power every step of the way, you can have a life beyond your best dreams.

That's what the apostle Paul is saying in that verse at the beginning of the chapter: Keep on keeping on; Don't quit. Even when life gets tough or doing right doesn't seem to be paying off, keep going. You'll see that things turn out better when you follow God. Paul earned the right to say those words. Many times he was chained up in a jail cell because he was trying to share God's message, and some people just didn't want him to set others free with God's Word. He survived brutal beatings. He also survived a shipwreck and a bite from a poisonous snake. Beyond all that, he had some type of physical condition that tormented him so much that he begged God three times to take it away. So don't think Paul was a privileged adult living a comfortable life telling you to keep going. Nope. Paul was in the middle of the battle when he wrote these words. He was a true survivor.

What got Paul through his challenges, and what'll get you through, too, is relying on God's strength. In the book of Isaiah, God promises, "When you pass through the waters, I will be with you; and through the rivers, they shall not overflow you" (Isaiah 43:2 NKJV). Whatever you go through, God will be with you, loving you, listening to you, encouraging you, and giving you the spiritual strength to endure.

The Choice Is Yours

Have you ever heard the expression "A penny for your thoughts"? Well, if someone actually makes you that offer, you should take him or her up on it. You could get rich pretty quickly. Over the next twenty-four hours, your mind could generate as many as 50,000 thoughts, often several at a time. So one day's worth of thoughts could bring you five hundred dollars!

The problem is that many of those thoughts aren't worth even a penny. Today, if we aren't careful, our thoughts can be sparked by images on the Internet or TV, bad advice, and careless talk from celebrities. If you're like most people today, you're often "connected." You have instant messenger, instant pictures, instant information—right at your fingertips. If we're not careful, all of this instant information can fill our minds with thoughts that are not helpful. We are so used to reading the next message, the next social feed, that we don't have time to think of God's messages; we don't have time to read and think about God's Word or pray. So we don't have much strength to fight the battle that's going on inside. We have let any old information enter into our minds "instantly" and we find ourselves thinking unhealthy thoughts.

Good and right thoughts, however, take effort. You have to choose to think God's way, then continue to choose right thoughts every day and every night. Remember that interview with Terrence, the former drug addict? He said that the process of becoming a new person was something he worked on every day.

Think of it this way: If you want to get out of shape physically, you really don't have to do anything. Just sitting around and eating whatever junk food happens to be handy will soon make you out of shape.

But to be healthy and strong takes vigilant effort. You must think about what you're going to eat and what to avoid. You have to make smart food choices. You can't allow yourself to fall into careless eating habits every day. And you have to discipline yourself to exercise, to make it a priority in your life. You're going to have to do things when you don't feel like it. Ask any real athlete: They don't always feel like practicing or running drills, but they do it because they know that's what it takes to be good.

Your mind deserves the same kind of attention—in fact, it deserves even more attention. You will face many choices in life. God wants you to make the right choices, and that starts in your mind. Your thoughts become your words; your thoughts become your actions. Your thoughts become your life. So choose life affirming, life-generating thoughts. When you do, positive words and positive actions will follow. Live your life expecting the best, not fearing the worst. And remember that you are not alone. Keep telling yourself, "I won't give up, because God is on my side. He loves me, and He will always help me." Remember forever this promise from the Bible: "The Lord is watching his children, listening to their prayers" (I Peter 3:12 TLB).

Don't Give Up! A Mind Isn't Built in a Day

As you strive to persevere and think and act the right way, sometimes you will get discouraged. That shouldn't be a surprise. Remember, you're trying to reprogram a mind, and that can take some time. Whenever you are sick, you usually have to rest or take it easy until you feel better. You may need to take medicine or see a doctor. But as you start to feel better, you slowly start to do the things you used to do. You don't just rush in and pick up full speed the day you feel better. It's a process to return to your healthy self. And it's a process to get your mind healthy. You have to take your medicine (the Word of God) faithfully, and slowly you will see your mind change. You will have to be patient and learn new ways to think; you may need to find new friends to be around—friends who are also trying to follow God's Word. But, if you do not give up, you will see a difference. With God's help, you can reprogram your mind and your thoughts.

Sometimes this process takes time, but I promise you this: It's worth it.

The Power of the Positive

I will meditate on Your precepts and have respect to Your
ways [the paths of life marked out by Your law].
Psalm 119:15 AMP

Life isn't easy, but it can be simple. Positive minds—filled with hope and faith in God and God's promises—produce positive lives. Negative minds—filled with anger and unforgiveness, to name a few—produce negative lives. Your mind really does have a lot to do with how you live. That's why it is so important to take your thoughts captive—to know what's really going on in your mind and to catch anything that is not godly before it blows up and impacts your actions.

One of the ways you can have a hard time winning the battle in your mind is when you are dealing with fear and doubt. Think about it: Are you afraid to hope? Are you afraid to imagine what cool things might happen in your life because you can't face the disappointment of seeing those hopes crumble? A lot of people feel that way. They have been disappointed so many times that they don't want to open themselves up to another hurt. They are living life by playing defense all of the time. Their focus is protect, protect, protect. They've already made up their minds that they need to be afraid to dream and hope because of their past or because of what they *think* may happen in the future.

It's understandable that people want to avoid the pain of disappointment, but let's go back to that key verse, Proverbs 23:7: "For as [a person] thinks in his heart, so is he" (NIV).

I want to confess something to you: Years ago, I was an extremely negative person. If you've seen me on TV or heard me speak, you might find this hard to believe, but it's true. I used to say, "If I thought two positive thoughts in a row, my brain would cramp up!" Here was my life philosophy: "If you don't expect anything good to happen, then you won't be disappointed when it doesn't."

As you might imagine, I was no fun to be around. I thought the way I did because I had endured so many disappointments in life, including being abused and not being able to go to college. These disappointments colored my whole outlook on life. My thoughts were negative; my words were negative. My whole life was negative.

To try and pull myself out of the quicksand of negativity, I began to seriously study God's Word. I prayed that God would restore me, restore my soul. As I made these efforts, I realized that my negative attitude toward life had to go.

I focused on verses like Matthew 8:13, in which Jesus tells us that as we think and believe, "it will be done for us..." This made perfect sense. Every belief had was negative, so it was no wonder that negative things happened to me all the time.

Now it's important to point out that Jesus isn't saying that you can get anything you want just by thinking about it. He is God, not your personal genie in a bottle. But He does have a perfect plan for you. And that plan isn't for you to go through your life depressed and discouraged. Jesus proclaimed, "I have come that they may have life, and that they may have it more abundantly" (John 10:10 NIUV).

If you don't have a clue what God wants you to do with your life at this point, that's okay. Pray to Him about it. Say, "God, I don't know what Your plan is for me, but I know that You love me and that whatever You do with my life, it'll be good. Please guide me in the abundant life I know You want me to live."

Then practice being positive in each situation that arises in your life. That won't be easy, because not everything that happens to you will be positive; not everything will be good. But you can expect God to bring good out of even bad circumstances. He can even bring joy out of sad circumstances. He can show you how to enjoy each day—even in the midst of difficulty or during times you are wondering where life is leading you.

Now, I know that the whole "when life gives you lemons, make lemonade" thing looks good on paper. But does it work in real life? Can God really work all things for good, as He promises in Romans 8:28?

Ask any follower of Jesus to tell you about their journey; I bet whomever you choose will tell you that they had to overcome some difficulty—whether it was a setback, a loss, or a challenge. But somehow, what they went through helped them get to another place, perhaps a place they had no idea was awaiting them. The woman who was bullied in school started an organization to help bring awareness to the problem. Her being bullied wasn't good, but her organization was, and it helped many people. Perhaps the child who had cancer taught her class how to persevere and gave her parents new purpose in life. Of course, having cancer was not good; in fact, it was downright awful, but something better than the cancer came out of the experience.

True faith looks for the good in those situations; true faith waits for the good in those situations even if the believer can't see the good just yet. True faith remembers Romans 8:28 no matter what. God really can work all things together for our good. It's a promise.

And one last thing on this topic: If you tend to be a negative person, don't feel bad about it. Don't feel condemned (that's basically beating yourself up over it), because condemnation itself is negative. Instead of beating yourself up, recognize the problem and begin to trust God to restore you, to show you the way out of your dark tunnel.

A New Day!

Therefore, if any person is [engrafted] in Christ (the Messiah) he is a new creation (a new creature altogether); the old [previous moral and spiritual condition] has passed away. Behold, the fresh and new has come!
2 Corinthians 5:17 AMP

Even if you have been a negative person in the past, you don't have to remain a negative person. If you believe in Christ, you are a new person, a new creation. You don't have to let the stuff that happened to you in the past keep dragging you down. You can have a whole new kind of life. You can have your mind renewed by the power and wisdom of God's Word. So take heart: Good things are going to happen to you.

One of the hardest things about being set free from the prison of negativity is facing the truth: "I've been a negative person, but I want to change. I don't have the power to change myself, but I believe God will change me as I trust Him. This will take time, but I'm not going to get discouraged with myself. God has begun a good work in me, and He is well able to bring it to full completion" (see Philippians 1:6)

God's Holy Spirit, living inside you, is key to these things happening in your life. If you are willing to listen, the Holy Spirit will warn you each time you start sinking back into negativity, kind of like that "Empty" light in your car that comes on when your tank is nearly dry. Pay attention to the warning. Ask God for help. Don't think you can handle this yourself. Let Him fill you back up and get moving once again.

Here's something interesting that will happen to you as you let God transform the negative you into a more positive version: You will notice negativity in other people, and you won't like it. You'll wonder, *Was I really that negative once?* It's like this: I smoked cigarettes for many years before finally quitting. But once I quit, I couldn't even stand the smell of cigarettes.

I'm the same way toward negativity. I was a very negative person. I could walk into a beautiful new home that was immaculately decorated and notice the one corner of wallpaper that was coming loose or the one tiny smudge on a window. Now I can't stand negativism. It's almost offensive to me.

It's important to note here that being positive doesn't equal being unrealistic, with a big silly grin on our faces all the time. If you have the flu, don't say, " 'I'm not sick at all," or "I really like having a burning fever and puking in the toilet all day; it's fun!

Don't deny the truth, but *do* stay positive. Say, "I believe God is going to heal me; this bug isn't going to hold me down for long." Isn't that better than, " 'I'll never feel better. In fact, I'll probably get worse and end up in the hospital."

In other words, strive for balance in life. Have a "ready mind," one that is prepared to keep life in perspective and deal effectively with whatever happens. Remembering to talk to God constantly can help your focus stay positive. Thinking of God reminds you that you are God's child and that God is always looking out for your good.

Have you heard the phrase "ready mind" before? It comes from the book of Acts, chapter 17, which talks about a group of people who received information with "readiness of mind." This means having our minds open to God's will for us, no matter what that will might be. And continuously focusing on God can keep your mind ready to receive God's goodness.

Have you ever experienced the pain of a breakup with a boyfriend or girlfriend? Recently, a young woman I know endured the sadness of a broken engagement. After she and her boyfriend called off the engagement, they began praying about whether the Lord wanted them to keep dating, even though marriage was no longer in the immediate future.

The woman wanted the relationship to continue, and she sincerely hoped and believed that her ex-fiancé would feel the same way.

I advised her, "Have a ready mind, in case things don't work out the way you want them to."

She countered, "Well, isn't that being negative?"

No, it wasn't. Negativism would be thinking: *My engagement*

*is broken; my life is over. No one will ever want me again. I'm
unlovable, and I've failed at love. I guess now I'll end up being a
miserable old lady with thirty cats!*

Having a positive, ready mind, on the other hand, would produce this attitude: *I'm truly sad about this broken engagement, but
I'm going to trust God to help me deal with the aftermath. I hope my
boyfriend and I can still date. I'm going to ask for, and believe, that
our relationship will be restored. But, more than anything else, I
want God's perfect will. If things don't turn out the way I want them
to, I'll survive, because Jesus lives in me. Dealing with this situation
may be hard for a while, but I trust the Lord. I believe that in the
end, everything will work out for the best.*

This is how you face facts and remain positive. This is balance.

The Power of Hope

My husband, Dave, and I believe that Joyce Meyer Ministries
and the work we do will grow each year. We always want to help
more and more people. But we also realize that if God has a different plan, we cannot let that situation steal our joy.

In other words, we hope for many things, but more important
than all the things we hope for is the One we hope in. We don't
know if our ministry will continue to grow or hit a plateau, or
even diminish in size or scope. But we do know that, whatever
the case, God will always work things out for our good. So our
mind is set on God and God's will much more than what we
desire or hope for.

Some of you might be saying at this point, "Joyce, if you knew
my situation, even you wouldn't expect me to be positive."

If you feel this way, I want to share a story with you. In the
Old Testament, God promised a man named Abraham that

he would be "the father of many nations," that his descendants would be so many that you couldn't count them all.

There was only one problem: Abraham was about a hundred years old at the time, and his wife, Sarah, was ancient, too, way past the age for a woman to have kids. The Bible account goes so far as to say Sarah's womb was "deadened."

So Abraham sized up his situation. He was an old guy with an old wife, and they didn't even have many of the modern options couples have today. Human reason said the situation was impossible, but the Bible says that old Abraham didn't waver or distrust God's promise. He simply hoped in faith. He left the situation in God's hands, realizing that, humanly speaking, he had no reason for optimism. He knew it would take a miracle to have a child. Abraham chose not to be negative, like humans normally would be. He chose to wait on God and to believe God had a way to work things out.

The lesson for you? Even when things seem impossible, don't discount that God will sometimes step in and do something amazing. You shouldn't expect miracles all of the time. But it's okay for you to believe God for them when He has told you to do so. Miracles do happen for those who really believe. And oftentimes those miracles happen much differently than we have dreamed up in our minds... but God has a way of surpassing our dreams and giving us exactly what we need when we need it (not when we think we need it!).

Isaiah 30:18 is one of my favorite Scriptures: "Yet the Lord longs to be gracious to you; he rises to show you compassion." Meditate on these words, and they will bring you great hope. God is looking for someone to be gracious to. He wants to show His goodness. But someone with a sour attitude and a dark mind isn't going to experience this blessing.

Struggling with Unbelief

I t's confession time for me again: At one point in my Christian life, I began to struggle to believe certain things. I began to question whether what I was doing with my life and ministry was really what God wanted me to do. I sensed that I was losing sight of the vision God had given me for Joyce Meyer Ministries. As a result, I grew miserable. Doubt and lack of belief always produce misery.

Then, for two days in a row, a phrase came to me: mind-binding spirits. The first time *mind-binding spirits* popped into my head, I didn't give it much thought. But the words kept coming back to me.

Mind-binding spirits. And because I wasn't sure what that meant, I jumped into God's Word and asked Him to help me.

After only a couple minutes of praying, I felt a tremendous sense of relief, of being rescued from an attack on my mind. It was a dramatic feeling, and I was grateful for the sense of release God gave to me.

Now, you might be asking, "What in the world are 'mind-binding spirits'? Sounds like something out of a Marvel comic."

Think of the concept this way: Mind-binding spirits are like tiny seeds of distraction that are planted in your mind. In time, these seeds sprout into different weeds: doubt, insecurity, unbelief, and cynicism. They pollute and clutter the landscape of your mind. These dangerous weeds wrap around your mind, squeezing it, irritating it. You begin to feel miserable.

If you feel these kinds of weeds sprouting and growing in your mind, it's time to rip them out by believing and confessing God's Word. In John 8, Jesus promised, "If you abide (continue) in My word...you are truly My disciples. And you will know the truth, and the Truth will set you free" (verses 31–32 AMP).

In other words, God's Word can clear out the landscape of your mind and make room for new, healthy growth. That's what it did for me. Before I allowed my mind to be overcrowded with unbelief, I chose to believe that even though I was a woman from Fenton, Missouri, who didn't come from a high-profile background, God could still use me to bring good to the world. He would open doors for me, and I would preach all over the world, sharing the practical, liberating messages He had given me. I also believed that I would have a radio ministry, that God would bring health and healing to those in need, and that Dave's and my children would be used in ministry as well. I believed all of these things and many other wonderful things God had placed in my heart.

Then the doubt started to creep back in. After a while, I couldn't seem to believe much of anything. I began to tell myself, I probably just made up those dreams about a ministry. It probably won't ever happen. I began to think all of these things were too hard and too impossible to come true.

But after I prayed and thought about God's promises in His Word, those weeds of doubt vanished. And once they were gone, the ability to believe the best for my life and ministry came rushing back in.

Decide to Believe

Some people hear the word *believe* and associate it with an emotion. But while belief can carry emotions with it, it's more than a feeling. Belief is a decision, an act of the will. Belief is persevering and following God's plan even when our emotions feel differently, even when our minds lack understanding. Belief goes beyond understanding. It's following the conviction of your heart, even when your mind is lagging behind or arguing with itself. It's important to understand this true definition of belief, because our minds often refuse to believe what they cannot understand. But when you have made a decision to believe, you believe—regardless of what you feel.

Note that because God's ways are better and more just than our ways, and His understanding is so much greater than ours, it is crucial to believe what His Word says, even if we don't fully understand all of the *why*s and *when*s and *how*s. If you're reading this book at night, look at the lights around you. Do you understand all of the intricacies of electricity and circuitry that create the light around you? Probably not. But you can still enjoy it and benefit from the illumination. You don't have to understand everything completely to believe it. And God is way too awesome and complex for our human minds to grasp completely. But our belief makes us trust in this amazing and big God.

Think back to our Abraham story. If he looked only at the physical realities, the cold, hard facts as they were, he would have no reason to believe God's promise to him. But he believed God instead, and his belief was richly rewarded: He is the forefather of the entire Jewish people—that's a lot of people. God's promise has been fulfilled.

There are plenty of seeds the enemy wants to plant in your mind. But you have the power, through belief in God's Word and His love and power, to pull them out and keep them from taking root in the first place.

Teen True or False

Put your mind to the test with the following quiz...
1. Most teens who drink do so responsibly.
2. A significant number of kids are having sex by age thirteen.
3. It's not uncommon for a U.S. teen to have as many as four credit cards.
4. Most sexually active young people have condoms on hand.
5. The dangers of marijuana are exaggerated. It's really not that harmful.
6. You can't get an STD unless you have sexual intercourse.
7. Parents are a major source from whom teens get their alcohol.

[Answers to Teen True or False quiz]

1. False. Almost 50 percent of people under the age of twenty-one who drink alcohol binge drink, meaning they consume five or more drinks in a four-hour period (according to samspaydayfoundation.org).

2. True. According to a U.S. Centers for Disease Control and Prevention's Youth Risk Behavior study, 7.4 percent of kids have had sexual inter-course by the time they turn thirteen

3. True. Almost 20 percent of eighteen-year-olds have four or more credit cards with an average balance of between $3,000 and $7,000 ("Making the Case for Financial Literacy: Undergraduate and Graduate Students," Jumpstartcoalition.com).

4. False. While 77 percent of sexually active young men and women say it's smart to carry condoms, only 23 percent say they always have one on hand (ibid).

5. False. Young people who use marijuana weekly have double the risk of depression later in life and are three times more likely than non-users to have suicidal thoughts. One factor in these dangers is that today's mari-juana is twice as potent as that used by previous generations, and today's teens are starting with the drug at younger and younger ages during cru-cial brain development years. ("Marijuana and Mental Health: An Open Letter to Parents," theantidrug.com)

6. False. You can get an STD from oral sex, or even hand-to-genital contact (ibid.)

7. True. In a national survey of more than 700 thirteen- to eighteen-year-olds, "one's own parents," with their knowledge and consent, was named the number one source for getting alcoholic beverages. "Someone else's parents" (also with knowledge and consent) represented the number four source. ("Teenage Drinking Key Findings," www.ama-assn.org)

Think About What You're Thinking About

I will meditate on Your precepts and have respect to Your
ways [the paths of life marked out by Your law].
Psalm 119:15 AMP

What are the Internet, TV, and music rules in your house? Are there parental controls on your computer? Are there certain TV programs or entire channels you're not allowed to watch?

Do you hear "What's it rated?" every time you ask a parent to go see a movie?

Or maybe you have adopted some rules of your own. Maybe

you won't download music with parental advisory warnings or view certain types of movies.

If any of this sounds familiar, good for you (and your parent or parents, too)! As media content has become increasingly questionable, more and more people are being careful about what they watch, read, and hear.

Unfortunately, very few people apply the same kind of discipline to their thought lives.

Most people let random thoughts drift into their minds and spend valuable time considering them. Some thoughts are rather innocent, such as checking movie times or looking through what's new on iTunes. Others can be impure or devious. In any case, careless thoughts distract us from pure thoughts, positive thoughts that lead to a rewarding life, rather than a wasted life.

The writer of Psalm 119, quoted at the beginning of this chapter, understood the concept of "thinking about what you're thinking about." He said he thought about, meditated on, God's guidance. That means he spent loads of time studying God's character, God's rules for living.

Meditating on God's Word has its rewards. The Bible promises that the person who follows this practice is like a tree firmly planted near streams of water. A tree that produces good fruit and prospers. This kind of person, the Bible promises, will be blessed.

The Gospel of Mark puts it another way: "Be careful what you are hearing. The measure [of thought and study] you give [to the truth you hear] will be the measure [of virtue and knowledge] that comes back to you and more [besides] will be given to you who hear" (Mark 4:24 AMP). In other words, the more time we spend thinking about the Word as we read and hear it, the more power we will have to live out our faith. When we meditate (think about) God's Word often, our minds are filled with the truth. We are filled with words and thoughts that help us follow God and live godly lives. Our minds are ready to steer us into goodness. Our minds are ready to help us live positively and see God's goodness more and more.

For example, you've probably heard sermons and songs about caring for "the least of these." You might have thought, *That's a nice sentiment, a good idea. We really should care for people less fortunate than ourselves.* But then you get distracted and wonder what's on TV or what your friends are doing right now.

When this kind of thing happens, you have to discipline your mind. You have to meditate on God's Word, not just let it drift through your mind.

According to Webster's dictionary, the word *meditate* means to reflect on something, to ponder it, to contemplate it or to intend in your mind to do something. In short, if you want to follow God's Word in your life, you must spend dedicated time thinking about God's message to His people. You have to practice thinking about God's Word, just as you would practice for a sport, a musical performance, or a speech. And when you are tempted to start thinking about what's for lunch or your weekend plans when you have really set aside time to meditate on God, you've got to change your mind and refocus on God.

The book of Joshua urges people to meditate on God's law day and night (see 1:8). That's because this discipline is so important that it shouldn't be crammed into a tiny corner of your busy day.

Take a few moments right now to estimate how much time you spend contemplating God's Word and thinking about how to apply it to your everyday life. If you're like most people, your meditation time is tiny compared to your TV watching time, your cell phone time, and your time texting or checking social media.

Here's another question for you: Are you having problems in any areas of your life? If you are, an honest answer to the "how much meditation time" question might disclose the reason why. I know this from personal experience. For most of my life, I didn't think about what I was thinking about. I went to church for years, but never actually thought about what I heard. All the sermons, the songs, and the personal testimonies flew through my head without ever landing and making an impression.

I read the Bible, too, every day. But I never thought about what I was reading. It was just a mindless routine; I wasn't attending to the Word. I wasn't devoting thought and study to what I was hearing, and I wasn't putting it into practice.

Instead, I simply thought about whatever happened to pop into my head at any given time. As a result, my mind was filled with lies, and a bunch of nonsense that wasn't worth spending any time thinking about. These things kept my mind busy, but not in a productive way. So, even though I was a Christian, I wasn't allowing God to control my thought life.

I needed to change my way of thinking. Maybe you do, too.

A turning point for me came when God gave me the message that is the title of this chapter: Think about what you're thinking about.

A Brand-New Mind

Do not be conformed any longer to the pattern of this world but be transformed by the renewing of your mind. Then you will be able to test and approve what God's will is his good, pleasing and perfect will.

Romans 12:2

In the passage above, Paul assures us that we can follow God's good and perfect will for our lives if we have renewed our minds. How do we do this? We pray that God will help us follow His way of thinking. We meditate and concentrate on God's life transforming Word all the time. Meditating on God's Word must become as indispensable to our minds as eating is to our bodies and as breathing is to our lungs.

As we are renewed to God's way of thinking, we will be transformed into who God intends.

Let me note right now, however, that right thinking has nothing to do with salvation. That's right. Salvation is based solely on Jesus' death for you on the cross, and His triumphant resurrection from the grave. You trust Jesus; He saves your soul. You go to heaven because you accept Him in faith.

Oddly enough, heaven will have people who didn't live winning, effective lives on earth, people who strayed from God's plan for them. Why? Because they never renewed their minds according to God's Word.

For years, I was one of those people. I was truly born again, and there was no doubt I was going to heaven. But I really had no sense of victory in my life, because my mind was continually occupied by the wrong kind of thoughts. I wasn't living the type of life Jesus came to give me; remember He said He came to give us life and life to the full (or abundant life). You can decide to be a Christian who will go to heaven and enjoy God's promises *or* you can be the type of Christian who will go to heaven, enjoy God's promise of eternal life *and* live a good life on earth filled with joy, peace, and love. You can have a really good life on earth that comes only from truly thinking about God's Word and letting it change your mind-set. You replace the wrong kinds of thoughts with the right kind of thoughts based on God's Word.

What, then, are the right kinds of thoughts and how do you keep them moving throughout your mind?

Something to Think About...

Finally, brothers and sisters, whatever is true, whatever is noble, whatever is right, whatever is pure, whatever is lovely, whatever is admirable—if anything is excellent or praiseworthy—think about such things.

Philippians 4:8

Did you know that the Bible provided such detailed instruction on how to direct our thinking and actions? As you strive to think about what you're thinking about, use Philippians 4:8 as a checklist. If you're like me, as you consider a thought that floats into your mind, you might not even get past the first two qualities.

For example, suppose that you find yourself considering trying drugs for the first time, or taking your first drink of alcohol. So, you ask yourself, *If I do this, am I being true to myself, true to who I should be?* And right there, you have your answer.

But suppose you interpret the "true" criteria another way. You know a juicy piece of information about one of the girls in your class; she is pretty much considered a "mean girl" by everyone you know, so you'd like to share the information you got on her with others. They need to know this girl really isn't all she claims to be, acting as if she has the best of everything and that others should treat her special because of all she has. You know the information is true because you saw for yourself. So, while this information is true and you have reason to use it against the girl, try the next step in the test. Is the information noble—is it the right thing to do? And is it noble for you to spread the information about the "mean girl"? (One version of the Bible translates the word "noble" as "honorable.") I think you'd have a hard time justifying how sharing this "true" information is honorable. And you'd run into even more roadblocks if you went down the list in Philippians 4 and tried to apply those guiding thought principles to the situation. Do you see how efficiently Philippians 4:8 can guide your thought life and your behavior?

Use this method as you take a mental inventory of your life. Ask yourself, *What have I been thinking about this past weekend; how much of my thought life would stand up to the Philippians 4:8 test?*

If you test your thoughts like this, you will find yourself spending more time thinking about stuff that will build you up, not tear you down (and build others up rather than tear them down). If you're full of wrong thoughts, you will be miserable, just as I was. Your mind will drive your emotions and your actions, making you see the negative side of everything.

And here's something else I learned from personal experience: When a person is miserable and negative, he or she usually ends up making lots of others miserable, too. And the people you make most miserable are your family and friends—including your girlfriend or boyfriend—the last people in the world you want to bring down.

I'll close this chapter by addressing another lie that is used against you. The enemy wants to trick you into thinking that the source of your misery is what's going on around you. He wants you to think your circumstances and the people around you are making you miserable. But that just isn't the entire truth—regardless of your circumstances or the people around you. Much of how you act and feel is generated by your thought life.

The Philippians 4:8 Check-Your-Thinking Checklist

Confused about what to think about? Put your thoughts to the following test: Are they...

1. True
2. Noble
3. Right
4. Pure
5. Lovely
6. Admirable
7. Excellent
8. Praiseworthy

Here's the deal: No thing and no person can make you miserable without your permission. Some of the happiest people I know struggle financially, face a challenging home life, or battle some type of physical affliction.

For many years, I blamed my unhappiness on things other people were doing or not doing. I blamed my misery on my husband and my kids. *If only they were different*, I thought, *if only they would be more attentive to my needs and help around the house more often, I would be happy.*

Finally, thankfully, I faced the truth: Nothing my family did or didn't do could bring me down if I chose to have the right attitude. My thoughts, not my husband and kids, were making me miserable.

Let me say it one more time: Think about what you're thinking about. If you do this, it's highly likely that you'll uncover the sources of many of your problems. And once you do that, you'll very quickly be on your way to freedom and peace of mind. Focus on the good, and you will feel better and make better choices. Keep your mind focused on the right things and watch what happens.

PART TWO

Six States You Do Not Want to Live In

INTRODUCTION

L et me ask a few questions to get started. Where's your mind? What state is it in? Does your mind feel "cloudy"; are you consumed with fear, worry, or doubt? Perhaps you are fixated on a situation at school where someone said something rude to you and you're actively working on a plan to get back at them. Or maybe you've experienced all those things just this week.

Your answers to these questions will reveal that your mind can be in a variety of "states" at different times. You can feel one way in the morning, another way in the afternoon, and have a completely different frame of mind before you go to bed.

The reasons why? This happens because we aren't relying on the help of the Holy Spirit, and we're not immersing our minds with God's Word, letting it guard our mind and thoughts. The result is that our thoughts are all over the place—in a variety of mental states. You've probably heard your friends ask you these questions before: "Where are you? What space are you in?"

In this section, we'll look over a variety of mental states you might be experiencing or have experienced before. And because your thoughts can drive your emotions and actions, it's good to know what to do when you encounter any of these mental states.

The State of Confusion

If any of you lacks wisdom, he should ask God, who gives
generously to all without finding fault, and it will be given
to him. But when he asks, he must believe and not doubt,
because he who doubts is like a wave of the sea, blown
and tossed by the wind. That man should not think he
will receive anything from the Lord; he is a double-minded
man, unstable in all he does.

James 1:5–8.

Did you know that God is eager to give you wisdom and that all you have to do is ask? It seems like a very simple deal:

1. You need wisdom and guidance about life.
2. You ask God for help.
3. God gives you what you need.

But many people make this simple three-step process needlessly complicated. Some of them ask God for wisdom, but, meanwhile, they are already busy trying to figure things out on their own. Others pray to become wiser, but their prayers are halfhearted and double-minded, having two minds going in opposite directions. These prayers may sound a lot like this:

"God, I really need Your wisdom to help me make some good decisions about my friendships. But, on the other hand, you probably have more important prayers to answer than mine. Who knows if You're even hearing me now? Besides, I can't imagine myself ever being wise. That's not who I am. I always mess up, always make bad choices. I don't even know why I'm bothering to pray."

Does this kind of prayer sound familiar to you? Have you ever started a prayer by sincerely seeking God's guidance, then have gradually seen your prayer morph into a weak list of doubts and insecurities?

I know those prayers. I lived much of my life with a double mind. I didn't realize I was in a battle and my mind was the battlefield. I was totally confused about everything, and I didn't know why.

A Reasonable Proposal

One thing that added to my confusion was too much reasoning. Yes, you read that right. Of course, reasoning is often a good thing, but not always. You might be skeptical about this position, but stay with me here. I have good reasons for warning you about an overreliance upon reasoning, and I think you'll find them reasonable.

Reasoning occurs when a person begins to ask the "why" questions about something. Now this is a good thing with questions like, "Why did the smoke alarm just go off?" or "Why is my car engine making that weird noise?"

However, in other situations, the enemy can use your own reasoning power against you. God may be guiding you, inspiring you to do something, but because it doesn't make sense or seem logical, you might disregard His prompting. The Bible warns us that when we are not open to God's Spirit, the things of God seem like foolishness to us (1 Corinthians 2:14).

You might have heard the story of the little boy trapped near a second-story window of a burning house. His father stood below the window, begging his child to jump. But the boy, because he couldn't see his father due to all the smoke, didn't want to jump. It didn't make sense to jump, but it wasn't until the boy trusted his father *more* than his own judgment that he was able to leap to safety.

Learning to understand how to balance the reasoning of the mind with obeying God can impact your life in ways big and small.

For example, one morning as I was getting ready to teach in a weekly meeting, I started thinking about a woman who helped us run the meetings. She had always been so faithful about her duties, and I felt like I wanted to do something that would bless her.

"Father," I prayed, "Ruth Ann has been such a blessing to us all these years. What can I do to be a blessing to her?" Immediately, my eyes fell on a new red dress hanging in my closet, and I felt in my heart the Lord's urging to give that dress to Ruth Ann.

First, a couple of things about this red dress: I had purchased it three months previously but had never worn it. It was still hanging inside the plastic bag I'd brought it home in. I really liked the dress, but every time I had thought about wearing it, I ultimately decided on something else.

It should have been a no-brainer to give this dress to Ruth Ann, right?

Wrong. My double-minded thinking hijacked my God-inspired idea. Instead of simply blessing Ruth Ann with a gift that God had conveniently placed right in front of my face, I started to reason.

I haven't even had the chance to wear the dress even once, and I really liked it. The dress was expensive, too! Shouldn't I get some wear out of this investment before just giving it away? And I'd bought red-and-silver earrings just to match the dress.

In the end, I reasoned myself right out of doing something kind for a deserving person. It took very little time, and within a few minutes, I forgot about the whole thing and went on about my business.

Weeks later, I was getting ready for another meeting at the same location as the one before. Again, I thought about Ruth Ann, and I began to pray almost the same prayer as before, asking God how I could bless her. I finished praying and saw the dress again. I felt weighed down by guilt. I remembered the previous incident, troubled at how quickly it had slipped my mind the first time around.

This time, there would be no rationalizing my way out of things. I had to face the fact that God was showing me what to do. I needed to either do it, or just be blunt and say, "I know what You are showing me, Lord, but I am just not going to do it." And I love the Lord too much to willfully, knowingly disobey Him.

As I prayed about the situation, I realized that the Bible doesn't say we can give away only our old, unwanted stuff. Sure, it would be more of a sacrifice to give an expensive new dress away, but that would mean the gift would be of greater value to Ruth Ann. God showed me that, in reality, I had bought the dress for Ruth Ann. That was the reason I could never bring myself to wear it. God had intended all along to use me as His agent to show kindness to Ruth Ann. But I had clung to my own ideas, until I was finally willing to lay down my ideas and be led by God's Spirit.

I have found that God wants me to obey Him, whether or not I feel like it, or whether or not I think it's a good idea. When God speaks, He wants me to act, not rationalize.

By the way, you might be wondering if I finally gave Ruth Ann the dress. Yes, I did. And she now works in our office full-time and occasionally wears the dress to work. She looks great in it. I'm happy I finally listened.

Who Are You Gonna Lean On?

Lean on, trust in, and be confident in the Lord with all your heart and mind and do not rely on your own insight or understanding.
Proverbs 3:5 AMP

It's significant that this verse from Proverbs mentions both the heart and the mind. The mind and the spirit can and do work together to help people follow God. You're using your mind to read these words right now, and, at the same time (I hope), the book is touching your heart—your spirit—as well.

Problems occur when people elevate their minds above their spirits (and by that I mean God's Spirit that is living inside of us all—individually). The spirit is the more noble of the two and should always be honored above the mind.

For example, let's say that you're facing a tough final exam in one of your classes. A fellow student hacks into the school's database, scores the answer key, and emails it to everyone in the class. Your spirit tells you that it would be wrong to cheat. In your spirit, in your gut, you *know* you should do the right thing.

But, let's see what happens if you start second-guessing and rationalizing...

"If everyone has the answers, it's really not cheating. Cheating is when you have an unfair advantage over other students. That's not the case here."

"I really need a good test grade in this class. It will help my GPA, which will help me get a scholarship, which will make me less of a financial drain on my parents."

"The teacher is lousy. I hate her style; it makes it hard for me to learn. I deserve some kind of advantage here."

"If I'm the only one who doesn't cheat, it's not fair to me."

"I'm a decent student. If I don't cheat and then get the lowest grade in the class, the teacher will be suspicious. I could get everyone else in trouble. I almost have to cheat, or everyone will get in trouble."

Do you see what can happen if we allow reasoning to detour us from following what God is leading us to do? Do you see the kind of mental gymnastics we can put ourselves through?

I don't know about you, but I want God to reveal things to me in such a way that I know in my spirit what I should do. I don't want to mentally run around and around an issue or problem until I am dizzy and exhausted. I want to experience the peace of mind and heart that comes from trusting God, not my own understanding.

You and I need to progress in our spiritual journey until we reach the place where we are satisfied to know the One Who Knows, even if we ourselves don't know.

The States of Doubt and Unbelief

At first glance, it might seem like the states of doubt and unbelief are the same. The two are related, and both can be equally dangerous. But there are some differences. Let's look at both doubt and unbelief, so that you can know exactly which one you're being lured or pushed toward.

The Dirt on Doubt

A great reference tool, *Vine's Expository Dictionary of New Testament Words*, notes that to doubt is "to stand in two ways... implying uncertainty [about] which way to take." It also says that doubt applies to one whose "faith is small [and one who is] wavering between hope and fear." Yikes. Basically, when we doubt we are saying our faith in God is too small or tiny to believe fully. We allow our minds to waver between belief and doubt, creating confusion and anxiety.

Here's a story that brings the definition of doubt to life:

A sick man wanted to be healed. So he prayed and quoted scriptures about healing. He believed that he would be healed. But all the while, doubts invaded his mind. This tension made him grow discouraged.

Then God allowed him a glimpse of the spiritual world. This is what the man saw: A demon was hurling lies at him, telling him, "You're not going to get healed; all of this reciting Bible verses like some kind of magic words; that's not going to work."

But the man also saw that each time he proclaimed God's Word, a light would come out of his mouth, like a sword, and force the demon to cower and tumble backward.

This vision made a profound impression on the man. He understood that it was important to keep speaking God's Word, because it was having an effect. And the very fact that it was effective was prompting the demon to use doubt to get the man to stop. Doubt is a tool of the enemy; it's not something from God.

The Bible promises that God gives everyone a measure of faith (Romans 12:3). He puts faith in our hearts, and the devil tries to negate that faith by attacking us with doubt. This is why it's so important to know and understand the Bible, to memorize key verses and be able to look up passages that build our faith. If we understand God's Word, we will recognize when the devil is trying to plant lies in our minds. If we repeat God's Word over and over, we can focus on God's promises and amazing ability. We leave less room for doubt to seep in.

Uncovering Unbelief

While doubt is belief tinged with second-guessing and uncertainty (the wavering back and forth), unbelief is a lack of belief or faith. Unbelief can even grow into an all-out rejection of faith. Unbelief is a dangerous state to stumble into, but it can be avoided.

Remember the story about Abraham, how God promised this hundred-year-old man (with an almost equally old wife) that he would be the forefather of many nations? Abraham heard God's promise, and Abraham's faith didn't weaken—even though he could have easily given in to unbelief.

As Abraham stood up to the temptation to disbelieve God's promise, the Bible tells us that he grew stronger in his faith; he felt increasingly empowered by it. This is a key point. You see, when God tells or asks us to do something, He also provides the faith and courage for us to follow through. He doesn't send you into a battle with no weapons or defense, shrugging His shoulders and saying, "Dude, I wouldn't go into battle unprepared like you are; Good luck, though. Let me know how it goes."

Instead, God gives us the ability to believe we can do what needs doing. And He'll help us get stronger as we turn to Him and His Word for wisdom and power. The enemy can't stand this. He knows how dangerous a person with a heart full of faith can be. That's why he does everything he can to weaken our faith. That's why he lies in an attempt to get us to stop believing. And these lies can be compelling.

Let me give you an example from the time that I received my calling from God to go into ministry. It was an ordinary morning for me, except that, three weeks previously, I had been filled with the Holy Spirit and was hungry to grow in my faith. I was listening to a teaching from a minister named Ray Mossholder. The teaching was titled "Cross Over to the Other Side." As I listened, my heart was amazed that someone could talk about just one Scripture for a whole hour and make it interesting the entire time.

Later, as I made my bed, I suddenly felt an intense desire come up inside of me: I wanted to teach God's Word. Next, I heard God say this to me: "You will go all over the place and teach My Word, and you will have a large ministry." And when I say I "heard God say this to me," I'm not necessarily saying I heard His actual voice, but that I could feel it in my spirit.

If you had known me at the time, you would have agreed with me that there was no logical reason to believe this was really from God or that I would be up to the task. I had a lot of problems. I did not appear to be "ministry material." But the Bible says that God can take what people might think is weak and foolish (1 Corinthians 1:27) and use it to confound even the wise. And He looks at our hearts, not our outward appearance (1 Samuel 16:7).

So, although there was nothing about the surface, "natural" Joyce Meyer to indicate I should believe God's vision for my life, I relied on promises like those in 1 Corinthians and 1 Samuel, and I was filled with faith that I could do what the Lord wanted me to do. I resisted the temptation to disbelieve God's guidance. When God calls, He gives you the desire, faith, and ability to answer the call.

I responded to what I felt God was speaking to me by investing years of study and training, waiting for the right moment to begin my ministry. And during this time, the enemy regularly attacked me with both doubt and unbelief. God's vision for me was planted like a seed in my heart, just like you'd plant a seed in a garden. While the seed is germinating and growing beneath the surface, the enemy works hard to get you to dig it up. He'll tell you it will never grow, or that if it does, it will only be a small, sickly plant that will embarrass you, so you might as well dig it up, or at least ignore it and not bother to nurture and water it.

If You Wanna Walk on Water, Get Out of the Boat!

If you attended Sunday school as a kid, you probably remember this story from Matthew 14:22–33: Jesus' disciples are out in a boat, a long way from land, when they get caught in a violent storm. The wind and the waves are kicking their boat around.

Then, early in the morning, Jesus approaches them, walking on top of the sea. This must have freaked them out, because they started screaming. They think Jesus is a ghost, come to terrorize them.

Jesus shouts over their screaming, "Take courage. It is I. Don't be afraid."

Peter, perhaps the most impulsive of all the disciples, shouts back, "Lord, if it's You, tell me to come to You on the water."

Jesus gives him permission, and Peter clambers out of the boat and, to his amazement, begins to walk on the water toward Jesus. But then he starts to panic. He looks at the strong wind and the churning sea. Peter takes his focus off of Jesus and thinks about the conditions. I bet he started to think: *What if I fail; what if I fall into the sea; what if the wind blows me down!?* Then, instead of continuing to defy nature and walk on water, Peter starts to sink.

But Jesus shoots His hand toward Peter. He grabs Peter's hand and holds him up. "You of little faith," He says, "why did you doubt?"

Then Peter and Jesus get into the boat. As they do, the sea calms, as do Peter's frazzled nerves

We can learn a lot from this incident. It took faith for Peter to get out of the boat. And note that none of Peter's buddies, the other disciples, wanted to take a turn walking on water.

But then Peter's mistake—focusing on the storm—caused him to doubt what he was already doing. Peter saw the wind instead of the Savior who was right in front of him. Doubt and unbelief pressed in on him, and he started to sink.

When storms come into your life, be strong. Trust in God's promises and His everlasting love for you. Storms will come into your life to intimidate and scare you, and the temptation is to focus on the circumstances, the "facts," not God's vision for your life, a vision that is bigger than any circumstance. The enemy knows if he can get you to believe you will fail or think about how impossible things seem, you will let doubt and unbelief stop you. But God can give you the power to overcome the doubt and unbelief. It starts in your mind. Review Scriptures, pray without ceasing and keep your mind focused on God.

Here's another example of how doubt and unbelief work: A friend of mine was confused when he graduated from Bible college. God had placed a desire in his heart to start a church in St. Louis, Missouri. However, as he considered his calling, he also took note of the fact that he had a wife, a child, and another kid on the way. And his entire budget to start his church was the approximately fifty bucks in his pocket.

The circumstances didn't seem to be leading him to a church. Meanwhile, he received attractive job offers to join the staffs of two large, well-established ministries. The salaries were right, and the ministry opportunities were many and enticing. Beyond these factors, he knew it would be an honor and a great résumé-builder to be a part of either ministry.

My friend deliberated over his three job options, and the more he thought about them, the more confused he became. His mind was assaulted with doubt. Right after graduation, he had known in his heart exactly what he should do, but now he found himself wavering. His life and financial circumstances didn't favor following his original plan. The two offers were tempting. What was the right thing to do?

He decided to ask a pastor from one of the ministries for advice. The pastor told him, "Go somewhere, get quiet and still, and turn your head off. Look into your heart; see what's there, and do it!"

Following the pastor's advice, my friend quickly sensed that his heart was in St. Louis and the church he wanted to start there. He had no clue how he would build a church with only fifty bucks to start with, but he moved forward, obeying God's call.

In 1980, my friend founded life church, where he has served as senior pastor for many years. Thousands of lives have been blessed and transformed through this church. I served as an associate pastor there for five years, and my Life in the Word ministry was born during my time working with this friend.

It is truly marvelous to see what happens when we follow God and guard the borders of our minds against doubt and unbelief.

God has a great plan for your life. Don't let the devil hijack your life. Don't let him steal from you the peace and fulfillment God wants you to enjoy. To see this plan come to life, you're gonna have to fight the battle within your mind and win.

Second Corinthians 10:4–5 says, "The weapons we fight with...have divine power to demolish strongholds. We demolish arguments and every pretension that sets itself up against the knowledge of God, and we take captive every thought and make it obedient to Christ."

The State of Worry

Maybe you've learned how to defeat the enemies of doubt and unbelief, the subjects of the previous chapter. But that doesn't mean the battle for your mind is over. This chapter will focus on the subtly dangerous state—worry.

You've heard of people being addicted to alcohol, cigarettes, meth, gambling, food, sex, and a host of other things. But did you know that you can be addicted to worry? That's right; there are people who are addicted to worrying over their lives, and when they can't find their own stuff to worry about, they'll start worrying about their friends, relatives, and neighbors. How do I know this? I was addicted to worry myself, so I am well qualified to describe this condition.

At one time in my life, I worried constantly. There was always something troubling me. As a result, I never enjoyed the peace that Jesus died for me to have. It's impossible to worry and live in peace at the same time. Think about it: Worry is defined as feeling uneasy, troubled, anxious, or distressed. Worry can also mean being plagued by nagging concerns. I have also heard worrying described as tormenting oneself with disturbing thoughts.

That last definition was key for me. It helped me decide, forcefully, that I am too smart to torment myself. I believe every Christian is too smart to fall into this trap (although many do). We just need to realize that worry never makes anything better. Never. So why waste time worrying?

It's the time-wasting, energy-draining properties of worry that make it so effective. If the enemy can keep your mind preoccupied with worries, you won't be using your mind in productive, God-honoring ways. And if you can think of all the ways something can go wrong, you've likely already lost the battle because you are frozen in worry and won't end up doing anything.

Jesus warned against worry. In Matthew 6:25–27, He instructs, "Therefore I tell you, do not worry about your life, what you will eat or drink; or about your body, what you will wear. Is not life more important than food, and the body more important than clothes? Look at the birds of the air; they do not sow or reap or store away in barns, and yet your heavenly Father feeds them. Are you not much more valuable than they? Who of you by worrying can add a single hour to his life?"

It might do us all some good to do some bird watching every now and again. We should note how well our feathered friends are cared for. They don't have a clue where their next meal is coming from or when they'll get it. And yet, I've never seen a cardinal sitting on a tree branch and having a nervous breakdown due to worry.

I know that dealing with low or poor self-image can be a real struggle, but surely you can believe that you're more valuable than a bird, right? And look at how well God takes care of them. What's more, our heavenly Father delights—yes, delights—in giving His children good things. But we won't be able to receive and enjoy these things if we are occupied by worry. If we focus on worrying about tomorrow, we can't live and celebrate today. We totally miss the abundant and fulfilling life Jesus himself said he came to give to us. (Remember John 10:10?)

Author Max Lucado titled one of his books *Grace for the Moment*. It's a good title, because that's how God's grace works in our lives. God's grace is always on hand to help us handle whatever we're dealing with now, at this moment. His grace for tomorrow will arrive tomorrow when we need it.

We've seen that worry is a bad state to be in, but what about the ways to combat it?

Here are a few great ones:

1. **Speaking the Word.** I highly recommend speaking God's Word out loud when you feel worry and it tries to make you focus on undesirable outcomes. It may not seem or feel natural at first, but give it a try. After all, the Bible is described as a sword, and, during an attack, a sword won't do you any

good in its sheath. You've got to take it out and use it. For example, you might want to encourage yourself with the words of Peter 5:7, "Casting the whole of your care [all your anxieties, all your worries, all your concerns, once and for all] on Him, for He cares for you affectionately and cares about you watchfully." There are two words you might want to say with extra emphasis:

Affectionately—God's care for you shines with genuine love for you. He doesn't care for you out of duty or obligation. He likes you; He loves you.

Watchfully—God is diligent as He watches over you. He doesn't get distracted or fall asleep watching over you. His loving eyes follow you wherever you go.

2. **Toss worries to God.** The enemy wants you to focus on your worries and stress; fortunately, you are under no obligation to hang on to them. Remember the verse about "casting anxieties" on God? Where you read that, you might have thought of "casting" in the sense of laying something at God's feet. That's a nice image, but it's not what the Bible means here. In this case, to cast worries means to hurl them like fastballs. Don't hang on to worries. Don't even say, "Next time I go to church or youth group, I'm going to hand these worries off to God. I'm going to lay them at the altar and give them to God." Don't wait—do it right now! Believe me; He can catch them, and He knows what to do with them.

3. **Rest in God.** Two artists were asked to paint pictures of peace. One painted a serene nature scene, with a still lake as its focal point. The other painted a tree branch extended over a raging, rushing waterfall. Perched in the branch was a bird in its nest, resting in the security of its home. The bird seemed to understand that in its nest, it was safe from the danger below.

I think both pictures can be used to remind you of the meaning of peace. The serene one shows how beautiful it is to slow down and focus on God's nature—a still lake. It reminds us of our Creator and the peace He brings. The other picture is probably more symbolic of life. We don't always get to live at a slow and serene pace, but that doesn't mean we cannot have peace. Even in the midst of raging water, we can know that we are safe. We can have peace because we trust and believe that God keeps us safe even in the middle of trouble. Our peace comes from knowing God. And just like the bird in the nest, we can rest safely in knowing that God loves us and protects us. The peace begins in our minds, where we think about God and God's promises. God won't remove all opposition from your life, but He can give you a sense of rest and peace during life's storms. So, rest in God's love and His plan for your life. He will meet your needs.

The State of Judgment

The teen years can be filled with lots of excitement, fun, and to be honest, insecurities, too. You're trying to find your way and figure out this thing called life (like most adults, too, but you are also stuck between childhood and adulthood, which complicates things). If you're lucky, you're getting the opportunity to meet many different people with different ideals, backgrounds, and thoughts about life. And, in the midst of this, you're trying to figure out who you are and who you want to be.

I think one of the best traits to develop is being a good listener who refuses to pass judgment on another human. When you allow other people to be themselves and speak freely, you can learn a great deal. And you can become a trusted adviser— even if you never give an ounce of advice. People need to talk through what they are thinking and can often do this best when they know the listener won't judge them for their thoughts. You can still be you while listening to someone with a totally different opinion on a subject. You just might learn something that you wouldn't have known or thought about without this person's perspective. But you won't get a chance to learn and grow if you're constantly criticizing others or judging them for their differences.

In fact, the people who go around judging and ignoring other people's opinions are called bullies. I'm sure you're familiar with the term. They want everyone to be like them and act like them. And they don't like it when someone challenges them or won't do what they want. So what do they do? They resort to bullying.

It's even likely you've experienced this firsthand. You may know exactly what it means to be bullied like this or in another way. But regardless of the way that you've been bullied or experienced it with others, know that God loves you and that He has an incredible plan for your life.

And if for some reason you find yourself on the other side of bullying—as the bully—I'll say it as directly as I can: Stop it. God has a plan for your life as well, and it's to remind people of the saving grace of Jesus and allow them to experience the freedom to be who God created them to be—even if they aren't like you.

I used to be a critical person. I was always able to see what was wrong with something or someone instead of what was right. Some personality types are simply more given to finding fault than others. Those who tend to be controlling often see what's wrong with something first, and they are quite generous in sharing their critiques with others.

I needed to realize, as we all do, that everyone is different. What might be the right course of action for me might not be right for my friend. I'm not talking about universal things like "Love the Lord your God" here, but rather the thousands of personal choices that people make every day. People have a right to make these choices without outside interference.

For example, my husband and I differ on our approach to a lot of stuff, such as how to decorate a house. If we go shopping for household items together, it seems like Dave always likes one thing, while I like something different. Why? Simply because we are two different people. His opinion is as good as mine, and vice versa.

This seems like an easy concept, but it took me years to understand that Dave didn't have something wrong with him just because he didn't agree with me on everything. And I wasn't shy about sharing just how wrong I thought he was. My attitude created a lot of friction between us, and it hurt our relationship.

Judgment and criticism like this are the fruit of a deeper problem: pride. The Bible repeatedly warns against getting too high-minded and having a high opinion of ourselves. If we are prideful, we tend to look down on others and value them as less than ourselves. We think our way is the only way; we think our opinion is, quite frankly, a fact, and things should go according to it. But an opinion is just that—an opinion. The Lord detests a prideful attitude that only sees things one way (our way).

Galatians 6:3 notes: "For if any person thinks himself to be somebody [too important to condescend to shoulder another's load] when he is nobody [of superiority except in his own estimation], he deceives and deludes and cheats himself" (AMP).

Suppose one of your neighbors comes to your door and says, "You know, I really don't like the way you look. You should dress differently and do something else with your hair. Your look just isn't working for me. And while you're at it, find some cooler friends. The people you hang around with are a bunch of losers. One final thing: Your house is ugly, too."

How would you respond? Have you ever been judged like this? Ever done any judging yourself?

I did. I used to entertain myself by sitting in the park or the mall and watching people go by, forming opinions about them by their clothing, hairstyles, companions, and so on. Now we can't always prevent ourselves from having opinions, but we don't have to express them and hurt others. We don't have to dwell on the opinions until they become judgments.

Also, I believe that we can grow and mature to the point where we don't find ourselves formulating so many negative opinions of the people around us. We can control more and more of this portion of the battlefields of our minds.

I frequently find myself saying, "Joyce, it's none of your business."

One great way to fight your way out of the state of judgment is to rely on the great counterweapon to judgment: love. You and I have the ability to love others and the command from God to use that ability. If we live a life of love, we protect ourselves from falling into being judgmental and prideful.

Proverbs 16:24 says, "Pleasant words are as a honeycomb, sweet to the mind and healing to the body" (AMP).

We all make mistakes, and we all have weaknesses. But instead of having a hard-hearted, critical mind-set toward others, the Bible instructs us to forgive one another, to show mercy, and to speak words of love and encouragement.

You'll find that if you focus on finding what's good in others and speaking "pleasant words," you won't have the time or inclination to judge them. And you'll find that as your attitude changes, your joy increases. Remember that every person you encounter has been created by God and is to be treated as such. Even if you don't like something about a person, you can still love them as you think about Who created them.

Jesus wants you to enjoy life to the fullest. Judgment, criticism, and bullying never bring joy. Showing love does. The choice is yours.

The State of Passivity

Have you ever been told, "You need to study/exercise/go to church clean your room," only to respond, "But I don't feel like it"?

Many people, even those who believe in God, are so passive in their approach to life that a mere absence of feeling is all it takes to stop them from doing what they should do. They attend church when they feel like it. They worship God only when their emotions are charged up. They donate time or money only when they're feeling generous.

Ephesians 4:27 (KJV) warns, "Neither give place to the devil," but many people don't realize a vital truth: Empty space is a place. In other words, a passive mind is like an empty and unprotected fortress. The enemy can easily overrun it. To win the battle for your mind, the enemy doesn't necessarily need your mind to be corrupted and filled with impure thoughts, motives, and lies. An unoccupied, lazy mind will do just fine.

For example, a person might tell himself, *I'm doing pretty well. I don't think bad thoughts about others, and I don't go around criticizing them, either; I just keep to myself.*

But sometimes, not doing something (or being passive) can cause problems. Staying silent—when we should have stood up or spoken up—can bring trouble, too. What if you saw an awful fight break out at school? Would it be right for you to stand by and "hope" no one gets hurt or would it be better for you to call a teacher to intervene?

Or what if you saw a friend picking on another student? Would you pretend your friend was doing nothing wrong, or would you try to talk to your friend, explaining how she or he is hurting another person?

In both of these examples, choosing to remain silent could be seen as hurtful and harmful, even sinful. Sometimes you need to speak up. Sometimes doing nothing is the issue at hand. Passivity is not always good.

Pulverizing Passivity

Years ago, my husband had a passivity problem. He was an active person in some phases of his life. He went to work every day and played golf on Saturdays. (He was also, as I've mentioned before, a disciplined Sunday afternoon sports watcher.)

But beyond these activities, Dave lacked motivation. If I needed a picture hung on a wall, it might take him three or four weeks to get around to it. This passivity created a lot of tension between us. It seemed to me that he did only what he wanted to do, and nothing beyond that.

Dave loved God, and so he asked Him how to solve his problem. God showed him that his passivity was part of the enemy's plan to distract him. In some areas of his life, Dave relinquished territory in the battle because of his struggle with passivity.

Dave was also passive when it came to studying the Bible and praying. I was aware of this weakness, so it was hard for me to listen to him and respect his opinion. I had a problem with rebellion anyway, so you can imagine how the devil used our weaknesses against us. Dave would tell me that I was always running ten miles ahead of God. I countered that he was ten miles behind.

Fortunately, God's Spirit revealed to Dave that he was giving in to passivity. Dave determined in his heart and mind that he would once again become a more active person in all areas of his life.

He began to wake up at five in the morning to read the Bible and pray before he went to work. The battle was on, and it was not easy. Sometimes, Dave would wake up but then fall asleep on the couch a while later. But even on these mornings when fatigue got the better of him, Dave knew he was making progress simply because he made the effort to get out of bed and strengthen his spiritual life.

On some mornings, Dave stayed awake but got bored with his studying or couldn't understand a particular Scripture. At other times, he wondered if his prayers were getting through. But he remembered what the Holy Spirit had revealed to him about his passivity and kept striving for progress.

Eventually, I began to notice that when I needed Dave to hang a picture or fix something around the house, he responded immediately. He became more decisive. The new discipline in his spiritual life was showing in other areas.

I must be honest and tell you that the change from passive to active was not easy for Dave. It took a matter of months, not days or weeks to overcome.

But Dave stayed with it, and now he is not passive at all. He is the vice president of Joyce Meyer Ministries and also bears full financial responsibility for the ministry. He travels full-time with me and makes the decisions about our travel schedule.

He is also an excellent family man. He still plays golf and watches sports a lot, but he does the other things he is supposed to do as well. Knowing him now and seeing all that he accomplishes, no one would ever think he was once plagued by passivity.

What Dave learned is that right actions follow right thinking. It's impossible to get from wrong behavior to right behavior without first changing your thoughts. A passive person might genuinely want to do the right thing, but he will never do it until he activates his mind and disciplines it to focus on God's Word and God's will.

For example, I know people—including teens—who want to live right; they want to keep their minds and hearts pure before God. Some have even asked me to pray for them. I tell them the same thing I told a man at one of my conferences. This man admitted that he was a prisoner of lust. He loved his wife and didn't want their marriage to be destroyed, but he couldn't keep his eyes—or his hands—off of other women. "Joyce," he said, "I just cannot seem to stay away from other women. Will you pray for my deliverance? I have been prayed for many times, but I never seem to make any progress."

Here's what God's Spirit helped me to tell him: "Yes, I will pray for you, but you must be accountable for what you are allowing to play on the movie screen of your mind. You cannot visualize pornographic pictures in your head or imagine yourself with these other women if you ever want to enjoy freedom."

And the same holds true for all of us. You can't entertain wrong or impure thoughts in your head and experience a freeing breakthrough in your life. Your mind cannot be a playground for sin. What happens in your mind will always influence your actions. It's not realistic to think that you can allow impure, graphic images to play through your mind (because of what you watch or think) and then you can turn around and resist the temptation to sin. Jesus makes this point well in Matthew 5:27–28: "You have heard that it was said, 'Do not commit adultery.' But I tell you that anyone who looks at a woman lustfully has already committed adultery with her in his heart."

A similar verse (Matthew 15:18–19) puts it this way: "But those things which proceed out of the mouth come from the heart, and they defile a man. For out of the heart proceed evil thoughts, murders, adulteries, fornications, thefts, false witness, blasphemies."

If you have a tendency toward passivity, take the initiative. Take action. Don't just wish that things will get better on their own, or as you mature. Make decisions. Make commitments. Plan to avoid sin. Every time a thought pops into your mind that is not godly, push it out and replace it with a prayer or Scripture or good thought. And stay away from watching or listening to movies and songs and conversations that are not godly and that you know will bring you down.

If you want to enjoy the good life God has planned for you, keep your mind focused on good things. Don't let damaging thoughts creep into your head, and don't play with them if they do sneak in.

If you truly desire victory over your problems, you must have a backbone, not a wishbone. Be active, not passive. You will act right as you think right. Don't be passive in your mind. Start choosing right thoughts, right now.

PART THREE

Damaging Thoughts That Can Derail You

INTRODUCTION

Now that we've gone through some of the undesirable "states," it's time to go further, to cover the specific thoughts and attitudes within those mental states.

If your head is in any of the places I'll describe in this section, it will negatively affect your inner life and your outer circumstances.

For example, I can recall a time when my circumstances were pretty good. Dave and I had a nice home, three lovely children, good jobs, and enough money to live comfortably.

But I could not enjoy our life because of some damaging thoughts and attitudes that I was holding on to. My life seemed like a wilderness to me because of the way I perceived things. I was dying in the wilderness.

All too often, you can have everything you need on the outside but still be terribly unhappy on the inside. Your circumstances may be near perfect, but you feel troubled on the inside. You don't have to live like that; you can allow God to shine a light in your darkness and lead you out.

I pray that this section will be a light to you, free you from damaging thoughts, and prepare you to walk out of your wilderness and into God's glorious light.

"I don't wanna take responsibility for my spirituality; isn't that what my parents and pastors are for?"

During his time in junior high and high school, a guy attended a certain church camp every summer. The camp always ended with an emotional fireside service, in which people could share what was on their hearts, confess sin, and ask for prayer.

At his first fireside service, this guy approached the flames and tossed in a pack of Marlboros. He tearfully related how he had been addicted to the cigarettes and that by "casting them into the fire," he was symbolically telling God that his life was no longer his own—but belonged to God.

The next summer, the same thing happened. The only difference was that the dude had changed cigarette brands over the course of the year.

Summer number three eventually rolled around, there was another fireside service, and...you guessed it. It actually became a sad joke among the other camp vets.

We shouldn't judge this guy, of course. It is easy to get emotional and full of good intentions when God first speaks to us and prompts us to do something or stop doing something. And many of us don't finish what we start, once the emotion goes away and we realize there's more involved than goose bumps or a few tears.

Many new "starts" are exciting simply because they are new. And that excitement will help you burst out of the starting blocks, but it won't get you to the finish line. It takes perseverance and a sense of responsibility to finish what you start.

The guy in our story wasn't able to take responsibility for his actions. The camp counselors and speakers inspired him. They motivated him to make a decision. But it was his responsibility to stick by that decision, and that's where he had issues.

There was a time in your life when you had zero responsibility. Too bad you were too young to remember it. It was when you were first born. Every single need was attended to by someone else. But as you grew up, you were expected to take on more and more responsibility. Right now, you might have a parent, sibling, teacher, or coach who does some things for you, but with other things, you're expected to take the lead.

It's the same scenario with God. He desires to teach His children responsibility. And the more spiritual gifts and opportunities He gives you, the more He wants you to do with them.

The Lord has given me an amazing opportunity to be in full-time ministry—to teach His Word internationally and to write books that are read by millions. But I can assure you that I have many responsibilities to fulfill continuously, which many people know nothing about.

Many people apply for jobs with us, thinking it would be the greatest thing in the world to be associated with a high-profile Christian ministry. Later, some of them are dismayed to discover that they have to do work here, just like anyplace else. They have to wake up in the morning, get to work on time, attend to their daily tasks, and follow the leadership of their managers.

When people come to work with us, I tell them up front that we don't float around on a cloud all day, singing worship songs. We work. We work hard. We work with integrity, and we do what we do with excellence. Sure, it is a privilege to work as part of a ministry, but I emphasize with new employees that when the goose bumps have vanished, we'll still be present, expecting high levels of responsibility.

God expects the same thing. He wants you to keep living for Him even when the goose bumps are gone.

You will probably have a few people in your life to encourage you on your journey with Christ, but they won't always be right at your side. Like a champion long-distance runner, you're going to have to be able to push yourself when there's no one else present to pace you or shout encouragement into your ear or yell, "Great job!" at the end of every run.

All of us must become motivated from within. We need to learn to encourage ourselves. We need to be able to push on when we want to quit—and we will all want to give up on a goal when things get tough or are just mundane. But we need to push ourselves to the finish line. We must live our lives before God, knowing that He sees all and that our rewards will come from Him if we are responsible enough to do what He wants us to do.

"My future is determined by my past and my present."

As you've read elsewhere in this book, I come from a background of abuse. I was raised in a dysfunctional home, and my childhood was filled with fear and torment. Maybe you can relate to this.

You've probably heard psychologists and counselors note that a child's personality is formed within the first five years of his or her life. As you can imagine, then, my personality—formed in major dysfunction—was a mess! I had to put up a brave front to hide my fear. And I built walls of protection around myself to keep people from hurting me anymore. I locked people out of my heart and, as a result, I locked myself in.

Here's another way I coped with my fear and hurt: I became a controller. I believed that the only way I could survive in life was to be in control. If I could control relationships and circumstances, I reasoned no one could hurt me again.

Does this sound like you or someone you know?

As I became a young adult, I really tried to do my best to live for Christ, to follow His teachings. But I struggled. The cloud of my past hung over me, making it hard to face the future with optimism. I thought, *How could anyone with my kind of past really be all right as a person? It's impossible!*

As I read the Bible and prayed, though, I realized that Jesus said He would heal the sick, the brokenhearted, the wounded. I was trapped in a prison in my mind, but Jesus came to open the doors and set me free. His specialty was helping people just like me. He gave me a positive vision for my life. He led me to believe that my future wasn't determined by what had happened in the past or what was going on in the present.

Like me, you might have endured a miserable past, and the circumstances you are in right now might give you little reason for hope. But I want to confidently tell you something: Your future can be filled with joy, meaning, and peace. I am living proof of this, and you can be, too. If you want Jesus to release you from the prison within your mind that may be caused by your reaction to your circumstances, trust and believe that He will. Listen for ways He tells you to overcome your issues, pray for strength, and do it.

Adopt a new mind-set. Believe that with God, all things are possible. Remember, He created the entire universe out of nothing! So if you believe you are nothing, give your nothing-ness to Him and watch Him work! All it takes is faith. Believe, throw yourself into His loving arms, and He will do the rest.

Here's one of the coolest things that can happen when you allow God to turn a dim, bleak past into a bright, shining future: You can break the destructive patterns that have plagued your family relationships.

If you've had an unhealthy relationship with a parent or step-parent, you can say, "This stops with me." For instance, if you have been constantly criticized and ridiculed, you can resolve to speak words of hope and encouragement to the family members you have now and the ones you will have someday. You can help create a legacy of light where there was once only darkness.

As you reverse these destructive patterns, giving to others the things you once craved (like love, encouragement, support), you will find that it's unbelievably healing to you.

"It's my way or the highway."

You might hear pastors and educators complaining, "Today's teens are more stubborn and rebellious than ever."

I suppose the question is up for debate, but throughout history, there have been many, many groups who could be strong contenders for the Most Stubborn title. For example, the Old Testament is filled with stories about the Israelites and their continued rebellion against God. So many times they defiantly turned their backs on God, then came whining to Him when they got into trouble. Then they would obey for a while, until their circumstances improved and they forgot how miserable they had been when they were living disobediently.

After a while, the Israelites would get cocky again, and the whole cycle would repeat itself. It's almost unbelievable that after experiencing great blessings and terrible punishments so many times that these people still wouldn't learn. But oftentimes, we do the same thing.

Maybe you can identify with the Israelites. You are good as long as things are going your way in life. And sometimes when things go well for a long time, you can tend to forget God or your promises to God. You start to do your own thing rather than follow God. Of course this leads to sadness and emptiness, which may cause you to turn to God again. But before long, the cycle of disobedience begins again.

I believe I was born with a strong personality, and I was destined to become a "do-it-my-way" person, no matter what kind of upbringing I had. But the years I spent being abused and controlled just added fuel to my rebellious fire. I didn't trust people in authority; I resented them. I became a person who resisted correction, disobeyed rules, and was difficult to manage. My attitude was simple: Nobody is going to tell me what to do!

Obviously, God had to deal with my attitude before I could become an effective leader. God can't shape clay that isn't moldable and pliable. I could not allow my past to become an excuse for resisting God's shaping of my life. To live the life of a winner, I had to show God prompt, exact obedience in all things.

As I worked toward this goal, I discovered that obedience is a process. As I laid aside my will and did God's will, I found my ability to obey was improving steadily.

It's important to continually improve our ability to obey,

because God requires our obedience in all things. We shouldn't hold back any areas of our lives from Him. We can't close any doors to Him.

Here's why total obedience to God is so vital. Most scholars agree that King Solomon, a man to whom God gave more wisdom than anyone else, wrote the book of Ecclesiastes.

Unfortunately, Solomon made many tragic mistakes in his life and spent much of his time being miserable despite his amazing wealth and power. Early in Ecclesiastes, he cries out, "Meaningless! Meaningless! Utterly meaningless! Everything is meaningless." (See Ecclesiastes 1:2.)

Later he goes on to list what he finds meaningless. Here is Solomon's Top 8 List of Meaningless Things:

1. Wisdom
2. Pleasure
3. Folly
4. Work
5. Advancement
6. Riches
7. Youth and Vigor
8. Everything (pretty much)

(And you think some of your friends are real downers.)

We can all learn a valuable lesson from Solomon. He was a truly wise man, and his wisdom was a gift from God. Sadly, he misused his gift. He made himself rich and powerful and surrounded himself with beautiful women, but he forgot to do one very important thing: humbly obey God.

Solomon wanted to do his own thing, live his own way. As a

result, he endured lots of needless despair, despite having every material possession a man could possibly want.

Fortunately, Solomon finally got it. Ecclesiastes ends with some great advice for all of us:

> *Now all has been heard; here is the conclusion of the matter: Fear God and keep his commandments, for this is the whole duty of man. For God will bring every deed into judgment, including every hidden thing, whether it is good or evil.*
> Ecclesiastes 12:13–14

I'll share with you my own words to express what I think this Scripture is saying: The whole purpose of man's creation is that he has reverence and worships God by obeying Him. All godly character must be rooted in obedience. Obedience is the foundation of all happiness. No one can ever be truly happy without being obedient to God. Anything in our lives that is out of order will be brought in alignment by obedience. Obedience is the real obligation of each person on earth.

Next time you're tempted to do things your own way, consider these words from Solomon. Obedience is each individual's responsibility before God.

Obedience becomes even more important when we realize that our choice to obey or disobey doesn't affect only us, it affects others, possibly many others. Think back to the Old Testament Israelites. Many of them died in the wilderness without ever reaching the Promised Land they sought for years and years. That's tragic. But what's more tragic is that many of these people's children died in the wilderness, too, as a result of their parents' disobedience.

The same kind of thing happens in your life. Your decisions affect more than just you. They can impact your family, your friends, your classmates, your teammates, and so on. And these effects can be positive or negative.

Recently, our oldest son came to me. "Mom," he said, "I have something to tell you, and I may cry, but hear me out. I have been thinking about you and Dad and the years you have put into this ministry, and all the times you chose to obey God and how it has not always been easy for you. I realize, Mom, that you and Dad have gone through things that nobody knows about, and I want you to know that this morning, God made me aware that I am benefiting greatly from your obedience, and I appreciate it."

What my son said meant a lot to me, and it reminded me of Romans 5:19: "For just as through the disobedience of the one man the many were made sinners, so also through the obedience of the one man the many will be made righteous."

Jesus provided the ultimate example of how one person's obedience can impact the lives of others. Think about how Jesus' obedience has impacted you and your family and so many others who decide to believe. By being obedient even to the point of sacrificing His life on the cross, Jesus saved the whole world.

You don't have to carry the weight of the whole world, but there are people in your life whom you can either lead out of the wilderness (of negativity, of rebellion, of apathy, or whatever) by your obedience or keep them wandering around as a result of your disobedience.

"Life is too hard for me to take; can't God make it easier?"

ere's a scenario that happens often in our ministry. A person comes to me for advice and prayer. I tell her what God's Word advises about the situation. She responds, "I hear what you're saying; God has been showing me the same thing. But, Joyce, what God wants me to do is just too hard."

God has shown me that the enemy often tries to inject this lie into people's minds, in an attempt to get them to give up. I used to believe this lie, but a few years ago, when God revealed this to me, He taught me to quit complaining about how hard everything seemed. He showed me that if I just kept obeying Him, things would get easier. He led me to Deuteronomy 30:11, which says, "For this commandment which I command you this day is not too difficult for you, nor is it far off" (AMP).

We tend to make things harder than they need to be by whining our way through them. Negativity zaps us of the energy and positive attitude we need to follow through on our goals. But God is beside us, telling us that His will is not too hard for us to follow and that the realization of the hopes we have is not as far off as it sometimes seems to us. But if our mind tells us otherwise, whom do you think we will believe? That's why we've got to keep our mind focused on God's Word rather than what we feel.

True, God might lead you down a hard road, with difficult footing and muscle-busting inclines. But He'll be with you every step of the way, giving you the strength you need—the mental, physical, and spiritual strength. Why would God lead you down a path He didn't intend to help you complete? Get your mind right (focused on God) and watch your path become easier to follow.

"Life is so unfair— doesn't that give me the right to complain?"

I studied these verses for years:

> *For one is regarded favorably [is approved, acceptable, and thankworthy] if, as in the sight of God, he endures the pain of unjust suffering. [After all] what kind of glory [is there in it] if, when you do wrong and are punished for it, you take it patiently? But if you bear patiently with suffering [which results] when you do right and that is undeserved, it is acceptable and pleasing to God.*
>
> 1 Peter 2:19–20

I tried to understand why in the world it pleased God so much to see me suffer. After all, doesn't the Bible say that Jesus bore my suffering and pain? If this was true, why was the suffering still happening to me?

Finally, I realized that suffering isn't even the focal point of the Scripture; it's the attitude one has about the suffering. If someone treats us wrongly, it pleases God if we handle it patiently. Think about those words carefully: God isn't pleased when we suffer; it's all about the attitude we adopt.

Jesus, again, is our example for suffering with a good attitude. Peter tells us that Jesus was "reviled and insulted" and "abused." But He didn't revile or insult or abuse anyone in response; in fact, He prayed for those who insulted Him. That's how He entrusted every circumstance to God, His heavenly Father.

Jesus suffered courageously, gloriously. He didn't complain, even though every ounce of suffering He endured was unjust. He is our example of how to handle life when it is hard and unjust. Is prayer your first response to insults and suffering?

Something happened in our family a long time ago that further illustrates the point of our attitude during suffering. Our son, Daniel, returned from a mission trip to the Dominican Republic with a severe rash and several open sores on his arms. He apparently had had a close encounter with the Dominican Republic's version of poison ivy.

Daniel's arms looked so bad that we knew we needed to get him to our family doctor. We called the doctor's office, only to find that our doctor was out that day. So we made an appointment with his backup. Our daughter, Sandra, made the appointment. She explained that Daniel was a minor and that she would be bringing him in.

Sandra made the forty-five-minute drive to the doctor's

office, only to be told by a nurse, "Oh, I'm sorry, but it is our policy not to treat minors unaccompanied by a parent."

Sandra explained that she had called earlier, specifically noting that she was bringing her brother in as she had often done, due to her parents' work and travel schedules.

The nurse stood firm. No parent, no treatment.

Sandra could have really let the nurse have it. She had added this errand to an already jam-packed day. Her brother was hurting and needed help, and it looked like she would be driving ninety minutes round-trip, all for nothing. The whole endeavor seemed like a big waste of time.

But Sandra remained calm and loving. She called her dad, who was visiting his mother at the time. He said that he would come over and take care of the situation. Earlier that day, he had felt led to stop by our offices to pick up some of my books and teaching material, even though he had no idea what he was going to do with them.

He arrived at the doctor's office, and the woman who helped him with Daniel's paperwork asked if he was a minister and if he was Joyce Meyer's husband. He told her yes, and she said she had seen me on television. They talked awhile, and Dave ended up giving her one of my books on emotional healing that he felt might help her. So two people's needs were met that day: Daniel's physical ones and a medical professional's emotional ones.

Here's the main point of this story: What if Sandra had lost her patience with the nurse and started complaining and protesting? What kind of impression would she have left with the medical staff? Think about the woman at the registration desk. What if she had seen me on television, talking about developing a positive attitude, while one of my family members went off on her in public?

A lot of people in today's world are trying to find God, and what we show them is much more important than what we tell them. Sure, we need to talk about Jesus, but to talk, then negate what we say by bad behavior, is worse than never saying anything in the first place.

Sandra bore suffering and frustration with patience—exactly what God's Word calls for. And Sandra's patience opened the door for a stranger to receive healing words from our ministry that day.

America: Whine Country?

Do you ever think the whole country is complaining? Have you noticed the long lines at various stores' customer-service departments and heard all of the grumbling that takes place when people finally get their turn at the front of the line? Have you read reviews online or looked at the comment sections for products, businesses, etc.?

In fact, take two minutes to go through any social media feed and the comments section, and it will become crystal clear that there is an overabundance of complaining.

There is so much grumbling and mumbling today and so little gratitude and appreciation. Do you hear your friends complaining about school, family, lack of money, and their "other" friends? Do you wonder if they complain about you, too, when you're not around?

I travel around the United States, and I want to tell you that there are people crammed into a homeless shelter right now, or standing in line at a soup kitchen, and they'd love to trade lives with these complainer friends of yours.

Have you heard one of your parents complain about "the

boss," "the long work hours," or "the lousy pay"? I know dozens of poor people who would put up with the lousiest boss in the world just to have a job, any job.

Philippians 4:6 advises us, "Do not fret or have any anxiety about anything, but in every circumstance and in everything, by prayer and petition (definite requests), with thanksgiving, continue to make your wants known to God" (AMP).

In this Scripture, the apostle Paul tells us how to face life's troubles: with thanksgiving in every circumstance. Notice how those words are carefully crafted. Paul isn't saying it's necessary to be thankful *for* every circumstance, but rather *in* every circumstance.

So you don't have to pray, "God, thanks so much for this broken leg. I really love broken legs. I've always wanted one. Hey, could You break the other one, too?"

Instead, while you endure that broken leg and the healing process, you don't focus only on your leg. You keep your life in perspective and thank God for all the things that are going well in your life. You thank Him that your injuries aren't worse. You thank him for the medical care and the help you receive while you heal. You look for things to be thankful for rather than things to complain about.

The Lord taught me this principle this way: "Joyce," He told me, "why should I give you the things you are asking for? You're not thankful for what you already have—you're filled with anxiety about them. Why should I give you something else to complain about?"

He showed me that if I couldn't offer prayer requests from a life foundation built on thankfulness, I would not get a favorable response. Neither will you. God does not say, "Pray with complaining." He says, "Pray with thanksgiving—every time."

Remember, true patience isn't just the ability to wait. Think back to those long customer-service lines. People there are waiting, but many of them are rolling their eyes, cursing under their breath, or heaving a heavy sigh every twelve seconds. That's not patience.

Patience is the ability to keep a good attitude while you wait. That's what Jesus did.

"My behavior might be wrong—but it's not my fault."

Have you ever heard yourself saying any of the following?

"I don't usually lose my temper, but my mom knows how to push all of my buttons till I completely lose it!"

"My teacher hates me—that's why I'm always getting bad grades and getting into trouble in his class."

"Some of my friends are a bad influence on me; I never get into trouble unless I'm hanging around with them."

"I didn't want to be sexually active, but my boyfriend has some kind of power over me."

"I didn't want to try drugs, but my friends just wore me down."

When we do something wrong—and especially when we do something wrong and get caught—we are quick to point a finger in blame. Unfortunately, that finger is almost never pointed back at ourselves.

I know this from experience. Countless times in my own life, I pointed a finger at my husband, Dave.

I vividly remember praying to God, asking Him to change Dave. I had been studying my Bible, and as I read, I noted various flaws that were listed and how Dave had a bunch of them. Dave needed to be different, I decided. And that would solve the problems in our relationship.

For example:

"If Dave didn't play golf on Saturdays, I wouldn't be so upset with him."

"If Dave would talk to me more, I wouldn't be so lonely."

"If Dave would buy me more presents, I wouldn't be so negative."

"If Dave helped me get out of the house more, I wouldn't be so bored."

Then the Lord spoke to me. "Joyce," He said, "Dave is not the problem . . . you are."

I responded maturely to this message: I cried and cried. I cried for three days straight, as God revealed to me just what it was like to live under the same roof with Joyce Meyer. He showed me how I tried to control everything, how I nagged and complained, how hard I was to please, and how negative I was. The list went on and on. The whole thing was a shock to my system and a blow to my pride. But it was also the beginning of a God-sent recovery.

I had fallen into the habit of blaming every problem on something or someone other than myself. When I acted badly, I blamed Dave. Or I blamed my abuse. But God told me, "Joyce, abuse might be the reason you act this way, but don't let it become an excuse to *stay* this way!"

What a freeing life revelation that was: *A reason doesn't have to be an excuse.* I didn't have to become a prisoner to my past and keep walking down the same path. What was done to me in the past could actually stay in the past. I didn't need to carry it around with me for the rest of my life, allowing it to influence my present and my future. The decision was up to me.

A key to being free from the Blame Game is to seek God's forgiveness. God is quick to forgive us if we truly repent, but we can't truly repent if we don't face the truth about our attitude and our mistakes. And facing the truth means going beyond just admitting we've done something wrong; it means not making excuses for that wrong behavior.

Here's an illustration: A neighbor called me one day and asked me to take her to the bank. Her car wouldn't start, and she needed to get to the bank right away, before it closed.

I was busy when she called, and I didn't want to be interrupted. So I was rude and impatient with my neighbor. I hung up the phone and realized immediately how terribly I had acted. I knew I needed to call her, apologize, and take her to the bank. But I found my mind filling up with excuses:

"I wasn't feeling good when she called."

"I was busy—she called at a really bad time for me."

"I was having a really rough day."

Deep in my spirit, though, I could sense God's Spirit telling me to quit making excuses. God revealed what I needed to do: "Just call her and tell her you were wrong, period. Say no more than, 'I was wrong, and there's no excuse for the way I behaved. Please forgive me and allow me to take you to the bank.'"

Saying those words was hard to do. My pride resisted. I wanted to run and hide from the responsibility, come up with more excuses and not face the truth. But you can't hide from the truth, because the truth is light. It will find you in any dark corner you try to hide in.

But don't be stressed about facing the truth. The truth will set you free to live the abundant life God wants you to enjoy.

I understand that something in your past or your present may have hurt you. It might be a person, an event, or some kind of circumstance you've had to live with. These kinds of things can be the source of a wrong attitude and wrong behavior, but they don't have to become excuses.

I know without a doubt that many of my behavior problems were direct results of the many years of sexual, verbal, and emotional abuse I endured. And I was trapped in destructive behavior patterns as long as I excused them on the basis that I was an abuse victim.

I'm here to tell you that you can definitely be free from your past, from everything that has brought you down. God promises, "I will never leave you nor forsake you," so hang on to Him and let Him lead you to freedom!

"I have a right to feel sorry for myself...my life is terrible!"

As I strived to leave the pain of my past behind and face the future with a positive mind-set, I found that self-pity was one of the hardest things to give up. I used pity for years, to comfort myself when I was hurting.

Then, during one of my "pity parties," the Lord spoke to me. "Joyce," He said, "you can be pitiful or powerful, but you cannot be both."

You see, the moment someone hurts us or we are stung by

disappointment, the enemy whispers lies to us, emphasizing how cruelly and unjustly we have been mistreated. We start to listen to the lies, and they wind themselves around us and make us prisoners of self-pity.

The Bible, however, doesn't give us permission to feel sorry for ourselves. In fact, one of the Bible's central messages is, "Focus on others, not yourself."

Recently, one of my speaking engagements was unexpectedly canceled. I had been looking forward to this event, and I began to feel deep disappointment setting in. At one time in my life, a cancellation like this would have hurled me into a deep pit of self-pity. While down in the pit, I would also have criticized the organizers of the event, judging them and having all kinds of negative thoughts about them.

But I have learned that in this kind of situation, it's best to step back and say nothing, rather than risk saying the wrong thing.

As I sat quietly, God began to show me the situation from the viewpoint of the people who had planned it. They had been unable to locate a building in which to hold the event, and God helped me realize how disappointing it must be to them to have their search fail. They were counting on the event—in fact, looking forward to it with great expectations—and now their hopes had been deflated.

I was amazed at how easy it was to avoid self-pity when I looked at the other people's side of things, rather than my own.

As Christians, we have a rare privilege when we experience disappointment. We can shift the focus off ourselves and our problems and think of someone else. We're not the only people disappointed, and we are not the only people suffering. In fact, we may find that others have it worse than we do—if we only turn our minds to think of them. God can give us a new beginning and a new sense of empathy—if we don't allow self-pity to keep us trapped in old patterns.

I wasted so many years of my life feeling sorry for myself. I became addicted to self-pity. It became like an automatic response to certain stimuli in my life. For me, when disappointment came, I responded with self-pity.

Instead of "thinking about what I was thinking about," I let wrong thoughts fill up my mind. And the more wrong thoughts that piled up, the more pitiful I felt.

I often tell stories about the early years of my marriage. During football season, Dave spent every Sunday afternoon watching football on TV. (And if it wasn't football season, it was some other "ball" season.) Dave enjoyed sports year-round. He liked anything that involved a bouncing ball and could easily get caught up in a game. He could get so caught up that he didn't even know I existed. As you might guess, I didn't enjoy any sport.

One day, I stood in front of Dave and said, "I don't feel well at all; I feel like I'm going to die." Without even raising his eyes from the screen, he replied, "Uh huh, that's nice, dear."

So I spent many Sunday afternoons angry and in self-pity. I would get mad at Dave and start cleaning the house. I was trying to make him feel guilty for sitting there and enjoying himself while I was being miserable. I would storm around the house like a cleaning tornado. I slammed doors and drawers, marched back and forth through the room where he sat, pushing the vacuum cleaner, making a loud display of how hard I was working.

I was trying to get his attention, but he hardly noticed me. So I would give up, go to the back of the house, sit on the bathroom floor, and cry. The more I cried, the more pitiful I felt.

After long fits of crying, I looked so bad that seeing my reflection made me start crying all over again. Then, finally, I would make one last sorrowful trip through the family room, trudging slowly and pitifully. Occasionally, Dave would look up long enough to see me and ask me if I was on my way to the kitchen and if I would bring him some iced tea.

The bottom line: The pity approach didn't work. Instead, I exhausted myself emotionally, often making myself physically sick as well. I wasted so much time trying to get Dave's attention because I was feeling sorry for myself. Imagine what I could have been doing: learning to enjoy life just like Dave was.

In time, I learned that only God can change someone. Believe me, nobody but the Almighty Himself could have discouraged Dave from watching so much sports on TV. And no one except God could help me see the error of my ways and help me to quit relying on pity to get what I wanted.

As I learned to trust the Lord and quit wallowing in self-pity when I didn't get my way, I saw Dave come into balance about his sports watching.

Dave still enjoys sports, but that fact doesn't bother me anymore. I just use his TV time to do things I really enjoy—instead of furious housecleaning. If I truly need or want Dave to spend a Sunday afternoon with me, I sweetly—not angrily—ask him. Most of the time, he willingly alters his plans.

Sure, there are still times when I don't get my way. But as soon as I feel my emotions starting to rise, I pray, "Oh, God, help me!" And He is faithful to help me every time.

"I'm not a very good person, so I don't deserve God's blessings."

We've talked about blaming others for the bad things in our lives, and a lot of people do that. But there's a flipside to the blame game. Some people blame themselves for everything bad in their lives. I'm not talking about the healthy habit of taking responsibility for your actions and reactions; I'm talking about feeling unworthy, so unworthy that you think you deserve every lousy thing that happens to you.

Sadly, many people endure double doses of blame. For example, a teen girl might hate her uncle for the way he physically abused her, but at the same time, she might think that there is something wrong, something impure about her, or she wouldn't have been a target for the abuse in the first place.

I used to think this way. I criticized and judged and blamed other people, but I also had a shame-based nature. I often blamed myself for the bad things that happened to me—even though a lot of it happened in my childhood, and there was nothing I could have done to stop it. I felt disgraced.

Grace is God's favor, God's power, given to us as a free gift. Grace helps us do with ease things we couldn't do on our own. Disgrace, on the other hand, comes from the enemy, not the Lord. Disgrace tells us, "You're no good. You should be ashamed of yourself for what you've done, for the way you think. You're not worthy of God's love or help."

Disgrace poisons your mind. You feel ashamed of what has been done to you, but you also feel ashamed of yourself as a person. This was how I felt. Deep down inside, I simply did not like who I was.

And sometimes, these thoughts can lead to very serious issues like eating disorders, self-mutilation, and cutting, to name a few. Don't forget, because there is a battle raging in your mind, it's your thoughts that drive your actions. And if you feel ugly and unworthy of anything good because of the shame and guilt you carry, you may be tempted to listen to the lies in your head and do things to yourself to pay for past mistakes or to ease the pain in your mind.

But don't believe the lies! God loves you and created you with a great deal of worth. He wants you to see yourself the way He sees you. That doesn't mean all the negative thoughts and feelings just disappear, but it does mean He will be faithful to help you.

And whether that's through prayer and studying what God's Word says about you or finding a great Christian counselor that can help you sort through your thoughts and feelings, take it one step at a time and hold on to God. Trust Him every step of the way, and start to walk out the road of forgiveness.

So perhaps the first person you need to forgive is yourself.

The beauty of God's forgiveness is that it allows us to respond to negative thoughts like: "You don't deserve God's blessings" with "I know I don't, but I can have them anyway!"

Here's the truth: Nobody deserves God's blessings. If they could be earned, they wouldn't be blessings. The book of Romans talks about the wages of sin being death, but the free gift of God being eternal life. Note the distinction between what we can earn and what God gives to us out of His sheer grace and love.

We aren't worthy of God's blessings. But we can humbly and gratefully accept them. We can enjoy God's blessings and have our minds blown by how good He is and how much He loves us.

"Why shouldn't I be jealous? Most of the people I know are better off than I am!"

According to the world's system, the winner takes all. If you can't be number one, you're a loser. The message we get so often today is, "Get to the top, no matter who you have to hurt on the way up."

The Bible, conversely, teaches us that there is no such thing as real peace until we are free from the need to be richer, stronger, more popular, better looking, and more successful than everybody else. We have real peace when we are content and are able to rest in the promises of God. We have real peace when we care more about pleasing God than pleasing ourselves. Riches may be nice, but real peace comes when our desire is to be true followers of God.

Have you ever seen how "reality" TV shows can bring out the worst in people? You get to see what they think about each other and how vain and selfish some people—even famous people—can be. When the camera is on in these reality stars' private lives, they are exposed, and many do not look like happy people. Their riches and fame have not provided happiness. Nothing outside of God can provide sustained joy. It's just not possible.

Sure, you should do your best at school, in sports, in music, or drama, or whatever your thing is. The problem comes when you can't enjoy what you're doing unless you win—unless you get first chair, first place, or first prize. You can't enjoy life unless you're the richest, fastest, best. If you become jealous or bitter every time you see someone who has something you don't, your life is going to be miserable.

I spent many years envying anyone who looked better than I did or had talents I didn't have. I secretly lived in competition with others who had ministries like mine. It was so important to me that "my" ministry be bigger in size and scope, attract more attendees to events, and boast a bigger budget than anyone else's. If some other person's ministry surpassed mine in any way, I wanted to be happy for that person—because God was blessing him or her—but something inside me would just not allow me to feel the way I should.

I remember when a friend of mine once received a gift from the Lord—a gift that I had wanted a long time. I didn't consider this friend to be as "spiritual" as I, so I became very jealous when she showed up at my front door, bubbling with the news of what

God had done for her. I pretended to be happy, but in my heart I wasn't.

After my friend left, I was shocked at the thoughts parading through my mind. I resented God for blessing this woman, because I didn't think she deserved it. After all, I had stayed holy, fasting and praying, while she ran around with her friends, having a good time. I was a religious snob.

God, however, had other plans. He knew what I really needed, while I was focused on what I wanted. He knew that I needed to get rid of my bad attitude much more than I needed a gift. God arranged the circumstances so that I could face myself and expose what the enemy was doing to my attitude.

Fortunately, as I better understood who I was in Jesus' eyes, I was freed from the need to compare "mine" with "theirs." The more I learned to trust God, the more freedom I enjoyed. I learned that God loves me and will do whatever is best for me.

What God does for me and what He does for you might not be the same as what He does for someone else. But remember Jesus' advice to His disciple Peter (see John 21:17–23). Jesus was telling Peter about some of the hardships he would have to endure in order to serve and glorify his Lord. Peter turned to his fellow disciple John and said, "What about him?" Peter wanted to make sure that if he was destined to suffer, John would be right beside him, enduring those hard times, too.

Jesus politely told Peter to mind his own business. He instructed Peter, "Don't be concerned about what I choose to do with someone else—you follow Me."

You'll find something amazing as you choose to follow God: He wants to bless you far beyond your desire to be blessed, but He also loves you so much that He won't bless you beyond your capacity to handle the blessings properly and to give Him the glory for the success you enjoy.

Back when I was jealous of my friend, God already had a plan for my ministry. He intended to make me steward over a ministry that would reach millions of people via TV, radio, books, social media, conferences, and more. But He wasn't going to bring these plans to fruition until I "grew up" in Him.

Take stock of your jealous thoughts and feelings. How do you feel when your friends post good news on social media? Are you genuinely happy for them or secretly wondering why they got a blessing that you didn't? Don't be afraid to be honest with yourself and with God about what you are feeling. He knows how you feel anyway, so you might as well talk with Him about it.

Whenever you recognize jealousy cropping up in your mind, have a little talk with yourself. Say, *What good will it do me to be jealous of a friend or classmate? God isn't going to bless me for being jealous; that's not the way He works. God has a plan for my life, and I'm going to trust Him to do what is best for me. It isn't any of my business what He chooses to do for other people.*

When you're done with this self-talk, try praying that those "fortunate" people you know will be blessed even more. Seriously. It's good for you.

I say prayers like this: "God, I pray for _____ to be blessed even more than she is now. Cause her to prosper; bless her in every way. I am praying this by faith, because I admit I feel jealous of her, inferior to her, but I choose to do this Your way, whether I feel like it or not."

In the big picture, what's the use of all the struggling to get ahead of someone else? As soon as we become number one, someone will be trying to topple us from our pedestal.

Think of sports. World and Olympic records are broken all the time. Teams that were championship contenders a few years ago languish at the bottoms of their divisions today.

God has helped me understand that "shooting stars" flash across the sky and earn lots of attention, but they're not around for long. He told me that it is much better to be around for the long haul, to hang in there and do what He's asked me to do, to the best of my ability. He, not I, is in charge of my reputation. Whatever God asks me to do is all right with me. Why? Because He knows what I can handle way better than I do.

Set your mind to be happy for others, and trust God with your life. Get rid of the jealousy that imprisons your mind and limits your happiness. Leave the possibilities to God. He will amaze you.

Think Like Jesus!

But we have the mind of Christ (the Messiah) and do hold
the thoughts (feelings and purposes) of His heart.
1 Corinthians 2:16 AMP

Several years ago it was popular for people to walk around with bracelets that had the letters *WWJD* engraved on them. The letters stood for: *What Would Jesus Do?* The point of wearing the bracelet was to remind the person to act like Jesus, especially when confronted with a difficult situation. Instead of going off or lashing out, the person would look at WWJD and be reminded to think like the Savior, not like a human.

I wanted to change that saying just a bit and ask: What Would Jesus Think (WWJT)? Of course, we should act the way Jesus acted, but I believe that starts with thinking the way Jesus thought. Which things would Jesus spend time thinking about, and how would He think about them? That's what we should be thinking about, too.

You need to think like Jesus if you want to act like Jesus. Now you might be saying, "That's impossible, Joyce. Jesus was perfect and all wise. I might be able to improve the way I think, but I'll never be able to think the way He did!"

You think you can't think like Jesus? Think again. You can do this. When God adopts you into His family, He gives you a new spirit, a new heart, and the ability to renew your mind so that you think as Jesus does.

Here's a look at this concept in action. Imagine that one of your friends hurts you intentionally—perhaps breaks a confidence or says something untrue and hurtful about you. Your initial, emotional response might be to get angry, maybe even start hating your friend and thinking about ways to get back at them. The results? Stress, tension, headaches, a sick feeling in your gut, fatigue, and sleeplessness, just to name a few. When you allow your mind to respond out of emotion, it can suck the life out of you.

On the other hand, as your mind is renewed and you begin to adopt the concept of thinking like Jesus, your response is different. Rather than focusing only on the injustice, you see things in perspective. You realize that God has blessed you and been good to you in dozens of different ways, so you don't let one incident overshadow everything else. In addition, you think of Jesus' loving, forgiving attitude, even toward His enemies.

Maybe you go to your friend and try to figure out what *actually* happened. You try to clear things up. And you don't repay evil with more evil. You pray for your friend, you pray for healing, and you live much more peacefully than you would if you were trying to get revenge.

Right Thinking in Action

When you adopt the mind of Christ, you fill yourself up with life, rather than let it get drained out of you. It's what I call "right thinking." Of course, you could respond out of emotion, you could allow your feelings to take over and go after those who have hurt you, but the question isn't "can you?" The question is "should you?" What does God's Word say about responding like that?

Right thinking is based on God's righteousness. Because God lives in you (so everything that is right about God is living inside of you), you can respond in the way He would. Learning to be like Jesus takes time and doesn't happen overnight, but I've come to thank God for that. He doesn't expect me to get it right from the start or to be perfect, but instead, He helps and allows me to grow little by little.

And as I learn more, as I learn how to think right, He gives me more opportunities to put it into action. For example, let's spend a minute talking about an issue you are likely dealing with: the way you think about sex.

It seems that just about everywhere we look in our culture, you can find something that has a sexual context to it. Whether it's the cover of a magazine at the checkout stand, billboards along the highway, ads or other content on social media outlets,

TV shows, movies...sometimes we can't avoid it, whether we want to or not.

Because it's so common to hear things about sex, we can be too casual about it and forget or even miss what God's standard for sex is in our lives. And whether you're a virgin or you've already been in a sexual relationship, I want to encourage you that following God's wisdom in this area is the best thing you can do. It's never too late to start living the way that He shows us in His Word. And His way is always the best for you!

So how do you develop right thinking on the topic of sex? Let's say you've been with your girlfriend or boyfriend for a while, and though you know you want to wait until you're married to have a sexual relationship, you're starting to think it doesn't really matter. You think, *What's the point? Who cares? I'm likely to marry them one day anyway, so why not have sex now?*

But I want you to take a moment to look at these questions—these are reflections of your thoughts. I know it can sound simplistic, but would God's Word (the Bible) line up with these thoughts? Because His Word is the standard or blueprint for your life, ask yourself if your thoughts about sex line up with His Word.

Again, I'm not saying it's going to be easy. You have thoughts and a desire for those things, and they were given to you by God, but His intention is for you to fully enjoy it with your spouse. So, although it feels like something is being kept *from* you, God is actually trying to help you stay pure *for* something.

Right thinking considers how you think and feel about something, but ultimately it turns it over to God. You can trust and talk to God just like you would a friend. If you are going through something—anything—be honest with Him when you are praying, and then trust Him to help you walk it out. Even if you've made a mistake, don't live there. Ask for God's forgiveness, dig deeper into God's Word and move on.

Now that you know God's right thinking is inside of you, how do you go about *actually* thinking like Jesus? Try these suggestions...

1. **Think positive thoughts.** Can you imagine Jesus walking around with a head full of negative thoughts? Could He have spoken so many uplifting, inspiring messages if His mind was clouded with negativity?

   Jesus was and is pure positivity, and if you and I want to walk with Him, we have to walk to a positive beat. I am not talking about forcing fake positivity into your head; I'm talking about having an outlook that remembers the good things when hard times hit, an outlook that expects the best rather than dreading the worst; an outlook that literally seeks out the good rather than allowing the bad to overtake your thoughts.

   Think about Jesus. He was lied about, deserted, ridiculed, misunderstood, betrayed, and much worse. Yet in the midst of all the negativity, He remained positive. He could always find uplifting, encouraging words to say. He always gave hope to those who approached Him.

   The mind of Christ is a positive mind. Therefore, any time we get negative, we aren't operating with the mind of Christ. Millions of people today suffer from depression, and I don't believe it's possible to be depressed without being negative, too. (I do understand that sometimes the cause of depression is medical/chemical, but even in these cases, negativity will only make depression and its symptoms worse.)

God does not want you to be negative. Psalm 3:3 says that God is our glory and "the lifter of our heads." He wants you to approach life with your head held high.

The enemy, meanwhile, wants to beat you down. And nothing will beat you down more than a negative mind. Life's problems can threaten to make you discouraged, but being negative won't solve a single problem. It will only make every problem worse. Positive thoughts, on the other hand, will bring light to the dark places in your life.

2. **Resist the negativity and despair that rob you of life.** Our spirits, empowered and encouraged by God's Spirit, are powerful and free. It is vital, then, to resist the feelings of despair and depression immediately upon sensing their arrival. The longer you allow despair to nibble at you, the harder it becomes to resist. Think of despair like a tick. You want to flick it off before it buries its head in your skin.

3. **Remember the good times.** In Psalm 143:5, the psalmist wrote, "I remember the days of old; I meditate on all Your doings; I ponder the work of Your hands" (AMP).

When hard times hit us and knock us backward, it's easy to forget all the progress we have made. Don't let this happen to you. Don't forget all the battles you have won, with God at your side.

Remember all that God has done for you and for others, too. The God who brought you to this point in your life is fully capable of guiding your present and your future. And as you follow Him, you'll pile up even more good memories to sustain you during the next challenging season of your life.

4. **Seek the Lord through prayer and worship.** If you follow the Bible's accounts of Jesus' life, one thing becomes clear. Jesus

was devoted to prayer. He prayed to God and thanked Him publicly, and He often withdrew from those around Him to spend time in solitary prayer with His Heavenly Father. It's important to note that Jesus didn't spend all of His time preaching, teaching, healing, and feeding people. If prayer time was important to Jesus, that's a powerful example for us.

God alone can restore you when you feel completely drained. Don't be fooled into thinking that anything else can satisfy you completely. God is eager to hear from you. He wants to meet your needs, and He wants you to spend time with Him.

Prayer, of course, isn't just a time for you to talk to God. It's a time to listen to Him, as well. Jesus sought His Father's guidance, reflecting the attitude of the psalmist in Psalm 143:8: "Cause me to hear your loving-kindness in the morning, for on You do I lean and in You do I trust. Cause me to know the way wherein I should walk, for I lift up my inner self to You" (AMP).

When you pray, allow God to assure you of His loving kindness; be attentive to what He tells you to do and how He wants you to do it.

Remember, a Christlike mind is a prayerful mind.

5. **Meditate on God and His works.** You don't have to be in a church to think about God. I enjoy watching TV shows about nature, animals, ocean life, etc., because they illustrate God's awesome power and endless creativity. They remind me how God is the sustainer of all life.

One of my favorite verses is Psalm 17:15, which says of the Lord, "I shall be fully satisfied, when I awake [to find myself] beholding Your form [and having sweet communion with You]" (AMP).

I spent many unhappy days because I started my morning with all the wrong things that might happen to me (and most of the time they didn't). I can truly say that I have been fully satisfied since the Holy Spirit has helped me begin each day with the mind of Christ. For me, spending time with God early in the morning is one sure way to begin enjoying the life that each day brings.

6. **Operate from a base of love.** When you're following the previous suggestion, make sure you devote some of your time to studying how much God loves you and what the Bible says about love. It goes so far as to say "God is love" (I John 4:8), but it's hard to know that if you never read it for yourself.

I remember when I began my ministry. Before the first meeting I conducted, I asked the Lord what He wanted me to teach. He responded, "Tell My people that I love them."

"They know that," I replied. "I want to teach them something really powerful, not a Sunday-school lesson out of John 3:16."

Then the Lord said to me, "Very few of My people really know how much I love them. If they did, they would act differently."

So I began to study the subject of receiving God's love. And I realized that I was in desperate need of it myself. The Lord led me to I John 4:16, which states that we should be conscious—actively aware of God's love.

Now I had a vague sort of understanding that God loved me, but God's love is meant to be a powerful force in our lives, just as it was in Jesus' life. As Jesus demonstrated, love can take us through even the most painful, humiliating situations and help us get through them (and come out better on the other side!).

I studied the subject of God's love for a long time, and as I did, I became increasingly conscious and aware of God's love for me. I thought about that love. I proclaimed it out loud. I learned scriptures about God's love and meditated on them, recited them aloud. I did this over and over for months, and the amazing truth of God's love became more and more of a reality to me.

Today, God's love is so real to me that even in hard times I am comforted by the "conscious knowing" that He loves me and that I no longer have to live in fear. I wish the same knowledge for you.

Let love be your base camp in the battle for your mind. Let it be a driving, energizing force for you.

7. **Be righteousness-conscious, not sin-conscious.** Many people are tormented by negative thoughts about themselves. They think God must be displeased with them because of all their weaknesses and failures.

   How much time have you wasted living in a state of guilt and condemnation? Note that I referred to time "wasted," not time merely "spent." That's because time spent thinking negatively is absolutely wasted. No matter the terrible state you are in when you come to God, He can make you pure and clean. He will forgive all of your sins. Second Corinthians 5:21 says that through Christ, we become the righteousness of God Himself. Ponder that concept for a moment.

   Christ enables you to be made into righteousness. You are right before God. So is everyone else who turns to Him. Let this knowledge drive how you think about yourself and others. Encourage yourself. Encourage those around you.

8. **Be thankful.** Jesus was a living example of Psalm 34:1, in which David proclaims, "I will extol the Lord at all times;

his praise will always be on my lips." He thanked God during the highs and lows of life—even at mealtimes.

We can emulate Jesus' mind-set and lifestyle by being grateful people, people filled with gratitude, not only toward God but also toward those around us. When someone does something nice for you, let him or her know that you appreciate it. Show appreciation to your family. Sure, they have faults, but don't take for granted the things they do right.

I have been married a long time, and my husband knows I appreciate him. But I still tell him how much I appreciate him. I thank him for being a very patient man. I tell him about his many other really good qualities. When we let people know we appreciate them, we build and maintain strong relationships with them.

I deal with a lot of people, and it continues to amaze me how some people are extremely thankful for every small blessing, while others are never satisfied, no matter how much is done for them. They think they deserve every good thing they get, so they seldom express appreciation.

Expressing appreciation is important. It's good for people to hear, and it releases joy in us as we share it.

So meditate daily on all the things you have to be thankful for. Tell God, "thank You." As you do, you will find your heart filling up with life and light.

If you believe God, you have the mind of Christ. I can't think of much better news to share with you than that. I hope the ideas in this concluding chapter will help you use that mind of Christ to ask yourself continually, "What would Jesus think?" Which things would Jesus think about? (Remember, if He wouldn't think about something, you shouldn't, either.)

By keeping continual watch over your thoughts, you can ensure that you won't just endure the battle, but you will win it.

You do have an enemy, but you have the weapons to win— weapons like love, like prayer. And your arsenal includes the ability to think as Jesus did, to have the mind of Christ. And something else to keep in mind: Jesus is always on your side— always fighting for you.

With that truth in mind, it's my heartfelt prayer that this book will help you battle successfully against every lie, imagination, or theory that stands against God. And I pray that your every thought will be guided by our Lord Jesus Christ, who loves you with an everlasting love.

If you have never accepted Jesus, I would love to pray with you now. God says in His Word in Romans 10:9 that if we confess that Jesus is Lord and believe in our hearts that God raised His Son Jesus from the dead, we shall be saved. Today, if you feel like Jesus is calling you to a personal relationship with Him, and you are ready to follow His leadership in everything that you do, pray this out loud:

Jesus, I know that I have sinned and am in need of a Savior.
I believe that when You went to the Cross, you went there for me, to pay the price for all my sins.
I trust You to save me right now. I give you my life.
Today, I know I'm saved and that You forgive me, but help me to understand what it means to live for You every day. Amen.

ABOUT THE AUTHOR

JOYCE MEYER is one of the world's leading practical Bible teachers. A *New York Times* bestselling author, Joyce's books have helped millions of people find hope and restoration through Jesus Christ. Joyce's programs, *Enjoying Everyday Life* and *Everyday Answers with Joyce Meyer*, air around the world on television, radio, and the Internet. Through Joyce Meyer Ministries, Joyce teaches internationally on a number of topics, with a particular focus on how the Word of God applies to our everyday lives. Her candid communication style allows her to share openly and practically about her experiences so others can apply what she has learned to their lives.

Joyce has authored more than a hundred books, which have been translated into more than one hundred languages, and over 65 million of her books have been distributed worldwide. Bestsellers include *Power Thoughts*; *The Confident Woman*; *Look Great, Feel Great*; *Starting Your Day Right*; *Ending Your Day Right*; *Approval Addiction*; *How to Hear from God*; *Beauty for Ashes*; and *Battlefield of the Mind*.

Joyce's passion to help hurting people is foundational to the vision of Hand of Hope, the missions arm of Joyce Meyer Ministries. Hand of Hope provides worldwide humanitarian outreach such as feeding programs, medical care, orphanages, disaster response, human trafficking intervention and rehabilitation, and much more—always sharing the love and Gospel of Christ.

JOYCE MEYER MINISTRIES U.S. & FOREIGN OFFICE ADDRESSES

Joyce Meyer Ministries
P.O. Box 655
Fenton, MO 63026
USA
(636) 349-0303

Joyce Meyer Ministries—Canada
P.O. Box 7700
Vancouver, BC V6B 4E2
Canada
(800) 868-1002

Joyce Meyer Ministries—Australia
Locked Bag 77
Mansfield Delivery Centre
Queensland 4122
Australia
(07) 3349 1200

Joyce Meyer Ministries—England
P.O. Box 1549
Windsor SL4 1GT
United Kingdom
01753 831102

Joyce Meyer Ministries—South Africa
P.O. Box 5
Cape Town 8000
South Africa
(27) 21-701-1056

OTHER BOOKS BY JOYCE MEYER

Joyce Meyer Spanish Titles

* Study Guide available for this title

By Dave Meyer

The BATTLEFIELD of the MIND
family of books
by #1 *New York Times*
bestselling author Joyce Meyer

Battlefield of the Mind

Readers will learn how to overcome negative thoughts with this multimillion-copy bestseller. They will gain control over their minds, become more patient, and conquer the damaging thoughts that try to steal their joy each day.

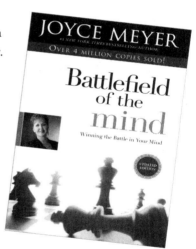

Battlefield of the Mind
Study Guide
(Revised Edition)

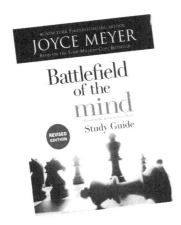

This thought-provoking, companion study guide will help readers maximize the power of what you learn in BATTLEFIELD OF THE MIND, with stirring questions, effective prompts, and designated space for journaling important reflections.

Battlefield of the Mind
for Kids!

Newly updated, Joyce's meaningful insights on the power of thoughts—delivered in a way that's just right for kids. Upbeat and filled with engaging stories, Joyce relates to upper elementary and early middle-school students, giving them the reinforcement they need for a crucial time in their lives and development.

Battlefield of the Mind
Bible

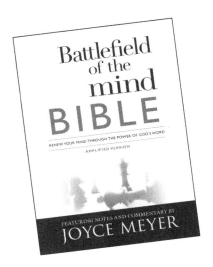

With notes and commentary based on Joyce's all-time bestseller, *Battlefield of the Mind*, this Amplified Bible and Joyce's reflections helps readers overcome the thought battles they face each day and achieve a life-changing sense of peace and joy. Available in hardcover, paperback, and beautiful Euroluxe bindings in blue, pink, and brown.

Battlefield of the Mind
Devotional

Daily inspiration and encouragement readers need to defeat the enemy and be victorious in the battle to transform their thinking.

Available wherever books are sold.